CONTENTS

While Impressionist painting of the 1870s is widely known today, the period leading up to it is much less familiar. The exhibition "The Origins of Impressionism," presented at the Metropolitan Museum of Art from 19 September 1994 to 8 January 1995, assesses one of the most important pictorial revolutions of the 19th century and demonstrates how it resulted from a gradual evolution rather than a sudden break with the past. Close to two hundred works by an entire generation of artists are presented together and thus form a highly representative thematic and chronological panorama of this decade. The essential features of the exhibition may be found in this special issue of the French art magazine "Connaissance des Arts," produced in collaboration with the show's organizers.

cover:
Claude Monet,
La Terrasse à Sainte-Adresse
(The Terrace at Sainte-Adresse),
oil on canvas, 38 3/8 x 51 1/8 in.,
98 x 130 cm, 1867,
Metropolitan Museum of Art,
New York; detail (see ill. 39).

1. Edouard Manet,
Sur la plage de Boulogne
(On the Beach at Boulogne),
oil on canvas, 12 3/4 x 26 in.,
32 x 66 cm, 1868,
Virginia Museum of Fine Arts,
Richmond; detail.

ABOUT THE EXHIBITION

Henri Loyrette explains to Sylvie Blin how the exhibition aims to demonstrate the subtle passage from Realism to Impressionism, while stressing the importance of the meetings and relationships that bound these artists.

Connaissance des Arts: There have been several exhibitions on the Impressionists these last years. How did the idea for another exhibition on this theme come about?

Henri Loyrette: Gary Tinterow and I had this idea while we were working on the Degas show which was held in 1988-9. We realized then how much the affinities between these artists in the 1860s must have stimulated their work and helped them develop and how they were able to benefit from the advances made by their elders. The 1989 Braque and Picasso exhibition also served as a springboard: these two artists' approach to working together struck us as an interesting idea that we readopted and modified to include a larger number of artists and to cover the longer period of the 1860s. We wanted to trace the relationships between these artists, to see how they worked together up to the emergence of their common style and subject range. This aspect had never been studied before, in spite of numerous extremely useful monographic or thematic exhibitions. The beginnings of Impressionism – the 1860s – had been somewhat neglected, partly because, in the case of artists like Degas or Renoir, it was a little-known period that only recent exhibitions have brought to light. Contrary to what has been said previously, we realized that Impressionism was not a sudden break with the past but instead resulted from a gradual evolution. We have tried to show how this movement took shape through the works of several painters, including Courbet. He was an extremely important figure to the Impressionist generation who, to some extent, measured themselves against him. One of the aims of

2

2. Manet's Portrait of Émile Zola *(oil on canvas, 57 3/8 x 44 7/8 in., 146 x 114 cm, 1868, Musée d'Orsay) has often been seen as the artist's manifesto; in fact it is the painter's homage to the writer who stood up for him against the Salon jury. The pamphlet that Zola published to coincide with Manet's 1867 exhibition on the Avenue de l'Alma is on the right, behind the inkpot.*

ABOUT THE EXHIBITION

the exhibition is thus to show this subtle passage from Realism to Impressionism. From the 1870s onward a legend built up around Impressionism: a certain Manichaeanism divided painters into "good" and "evil"; an over-simplified historiography that emphasized characteristics such as the use of lighter colors and plein-air painting, which were neither systematic nor prominent in the 1860s. In fact, during the 1860s, everyone sought success by traditional means and hoped for acclaim at the Salon; artists therefore tried their hand at all categories of painting – history painting, portraits, still lifes, and so on. But when they later chose to simplify their production, or to specialize, certain genres were abandoned.

CdA: How did you decide upon the period (1859-1869) covered in the exhibition?

Henri Loyrette: For many of these painters 1859 was the year of their first Salon or of their first attempt at being accepted. It's the year Monet arrived in Paris and Degas came back from Italy: it was therefore a decisive time, which also coincides with their discovery of the contemporary painting they would admire – Daubigny, Troyon – or disapprove of – Bouguereau, Gérôme, Baudry. It is also a date which enables us to compare the era's major painting trends. The Franco-Prussian War broke out in 1870, but it merely delayed the rise of Impressionism which had already taken root: 1869 is the year in which Monet and Renoir painted *La Grenouillère*.

CdA: This is another joint exhibition mounted by the Metropolitan Museum of New York and the Musée d'Orsay.

Henri Loyrette: As you know, we worked with Gary Tinterow and the Metropolitan on the Degas exhibition; it was a very satisfactory collaboration. Furthermore, our two collections together provide an extremely comprehensive and interesting panoramic view of the 1860s. Despite the diverse styles of the leading artists, the paintings in The "Origins of Impressionism" demonstrate the underlying coherence of this movement. Favorable and hostile critics of the day all saw the new generation as Courbet's descend-

ants and the ties that linked Manet, Degas, Monet, and others.

CdA: Could it be said that these young painters joined together in order to stand up to the critics' outrage?

Henri Loyrette: There were obviously strategic reasons not only for their united front vis-à-vis the Salon jury, the public, and the critics, but also for their determination to exhibit, either together or individually, outside official venues. They were helped by Courbet's example and his personal exhibition in 1855 was a bold experiment that Manet would repeat in 1867.

CdA: Unlike previous periods, in which major artists compelled recognition and could be identified with a style – Delacroix and Romanticism, Courbet and Realism – here a host of rather strong personalities make up the Impressionist trend. It seems impossible to point to one painter who surpasses the others and alone embodies this movement.

Henri Loyrette: That's true. The idea of making a choice is inconceivable today. But at the time Manet and Degas couldn't be ranked together, even if they were two very strong personalities. Manet had a reputation, unlike Degas who spoke of him as a "Garibaldi-type celebrity." Degas was still relatively unknown and, at that point, was neither acclaimed nor rejected as Manet was. They were not viewed in the same way. Manet undoubtedly played an important role, to some extent assuming the position held by Courbet in the 1850s. What the exhibition brings to light is Manet's extremely prominent, yet misunderstood role. He was not really the so-called pioneer of Impressionism but rather the embodiment of the passage from Realism to Impressionism. This however did not stop him from claiming to be the leader of Impressionism. Manet, in fact, only became an Impressionist thanks to Monet's influence.

CdA: Nevertheless Manet had a certain aura and exerted an influence, albeit more intellectual and moral than purely pictorial, over other, often younger artists.

Henri Loyrette: Yes, he occupies the place of honor, in the center of the group, in Fantin-Latour's *Studio at the*

4

5

ABOUT THE EXHIBITION

Batignolles, and Bazille's *Studio in the rue La Condamine*.

CdA: The growing changes in attitude apparently owed much to his influence, as his independence and intransigence served as a model for the new generation.

Henri Loyrette: That is so, but here again Manet appears as an ambiguous figure. He was very much a member of the establishment, striving for recognition and well aware of contemporary tastes. For a long time he moved within Baudelaire's sphere and kept up complex relationships with writers. Though it was Zola, rather than Baudelaire, who would reveal the painter's true character to himself. It is difficult to pinpoint individual roles, and it could be said that the writer and the artist had a mutual influence on each other. But Zola's influence would finally prove to be greater, and Manet's portrait of him could be interpreted as a personal homage to the writer. Moreover, Zola was the first to underscore both the various influences on the painter's work – from Japanese art to the painting of Velázquez – and the extent to which they affected it.

CdA: What approach did you adopt in mounting this exhibition? And how did you make your choices?

Henri Loyrette: We opted for a hanging that was both thematic and chronological. First we had to select the artists we were going to exhibit, as well as the space and importance we would give to each one. Certain figures, like Manet and Monet, emerge from the group and are very much in the foreground. Pissarro, Cézanne, and Fantin-Latour remain in the background, while others, like Whistler, have unfortunately had to be sacrificed. It was also a problem deciding which of the artists that counted would be put around them: Courbet was the most important, in all categories – the nude, landscape, genre scene – but Tissot, Daubigny, Boudin, Corot, and Jongkind will make occasional appearances as well.

CdA: Which theme was given priority? Landscape?

Henri Loyrette: Landscape and figure painting. Whatever themes these artists

6. Frédéric Bazille portrayed himself showing Manet and Monet his paintings in his Atelier de la rue La Condamine (Studio in the rue La Condamine in Paris, *oil on canvas, 38 3/8 x 50 3/8 in., 97 x 127 cm, Musée d'Orsay).* Le Pêcheur à l'épervier (The Fisherman with a Net) *and the early version of* La Toilette *can be seen hanging on the walls.*

F. Bazille 1870

F. Bazille. 1869

adopted, we in fact wanted to show how they all sought to produce a modern rendering of even the most traditional subjects, like the nude, the landscape, or history painting; how they treated classical subjects with a modern approach, as Veronese, for example, had done with *The Wedding Feast at Cana*.

CdA: Nearly two hundred paintings are assembled here. That makes quite an extraordinary gathering. But is there anything missing, or do you have any regrets?

Henri Loyrette: Yes, naturally, for all kinds of reasons, sometimes arising from the working practices of these artists who, in order to gain entry to the Salon, executed large-scale canvases, which today pose a number of transportation problems. We regret, for instance, the absence of Monet's *Camille*, painted in 1866 (Bremen), or of Manet's *The Execution of Maximilian* (Mannheim). But on the whole, museums, and especially the American museums, have been extremely generous: we have obtained substantial loans, including Manet's portrait of *Baudelaire's Mistress*, from the Museum of Budapest, Bazille's *Summer Scene*, from the Fogg Art Museum, Renoir's *Clown at the Circus*, from Otterlo. The presence of a number of these large figures in Paris is quite exceptional.

CdA: Works held in collections all over the world can thus be seen together for the first time.

Henri Loyrette: Yes, paintings that have never hung side by side before will be on view here, like the four *Grenouillères* and the three views of Paris painted by Monet in the 1860s. On the other hand, the differences between artists such as the Provençal landscapists – Guigou, etc. – made it impossible to include them. These painters, moreover, generally did not know each other. This is also true of artists like Boudin and Jongkind, who were overshadowed by more imposing personalities: their role is by no means negligible, but it does not warrant a very prominent place in the exhibition.

CdA: The 1860s will be more widely known and understood thanks to this event. Does it throw any radically new light on the decade or does it merely confirm previous analyses?

Henri Loyrette: I believe this period will no longer be considered in the same way as before. When these artists are studied as a group, instead of individually, certain obvious links can be established and therefore lead to a clearer understanding of Impressionism.

CdA: So the relationships between these artists and their meetings were very important?

Henri Loyrette: They were decisive in each painter's individual development. Despite the differences of background

8

and training, the work they did in common was fundamental. In Monet, Bazille, and Renoir, it's glaringly evident.

CdA: Was this collective working "method" a novel idea in the history of painting?

Henri Loyrette: In the years preceding this period, I can't think of any movement of this size that brought so many artists together; no equivalent phenomenon existed before 1860. Furthermore, all of these painters kept their promises,

7. In his Scène d'été *(Summer Scene, oil on canvas, 62 1/4 x 62 1/2 in., 161 x 161 cm, 1869, Fogg Art Museum, Harvard University), Bazille not only sets his figures in the open air but also approaches the nude in the same way as he would a genre scene, as an observation of real life. Despite its boldness, the painting was accepted at the 1870 Salon.*

8. Le Clown au cirque (Clown at the Circus, oil on canvas, 76 1/8 x 51 1/8 in., 192 x 128 cm, 1868, Rijksmuseum Kröller-Müller, Otterlo), portrait of the clown and violinist James Bollinger Mazurtreek, is one of Renoir's major works, which implicitly expresses his admiration for Manet.

so to speak; after ten years, they had all proved their strength with admirable force. No comparable phenomenon can be found in the previous decades. Perhaps what is most striking was their determination to keep searching, to always move ahead, and to look back at the path each one had trod.

CdA: Were the writers and intellectuals of the day as influential as has sometimes been claimed? Charles Baudelaire, who is regarded as one of the fathers of modernity, springs immediately to mind.

9

9. Renoir's interest in portraits went back to his early days as a painter. The models he chose were often members of his family or his friends, as in this: Claude Monet *(oil on canvas, 33 1/2 x 23 5/8 in., 85 x 60 cm, 1875, Musée d'Orsay).*

10. Bazille's rapidly executed Portrait of Renoir *(oil on canvas, 24 3/8 x 20 1/8 in., 62 x 51 cm, 1867, Musée d'Orsay) captures the atmosphere in which these young painters lived and the friendship they shared.*

Henri Loyrette: Baudelaire ultimately had little to do with the artistic life of those years. What he said about Manet was rather ambiguous, and he didn't even mention the others. Before 1864, the year Baudelaire left for Belgium, this movement wasn't easily perceived. It was only after 1865 that Zola, who took an interest in Manet, Cézanne, and Monet, first recognized the coherence of this new trend. It was really he who would best define the movement.

CdA: Whoever the protagonists were, whether painters or writers, didn't the debate on art and painting that now took place in cafés, instead of at the Salon or the Academy, go far beyond purely pictorial questions?

Henri Loyrette: The existence of a more general reflection on painting is incontestable. It wasn't exactly a revolution, but more of an evolution. Profound changes in the debate on painting and in literature alike can be discerned.

CdA: And finally how would you define this painting?

Henri Loyrette: First of all, as a simplicity of means, or the refusal to "fill out" a composition: on the contrary, things were both shown and named in a very simple manner. It was Olympia, not Venus. Mythological fancy dress, metaphors, and pompous conventions were set aside. Everything had to be rethought, even style. It was a new way of conceiving a painting: everything had to be painted in the same manner and was of equal importance. The background, the motif and the "accessories" all counted and anything superfluous was left out. The hierarchy previously found within a painting disappeared; thus Manet's "pantheism," particularly in his *Déjeuner sur l'herbe*, would be denounced by certain critics of the day. Though it was sometimes taken as a disdain for the subject, it was, in fact, a different conception that constitutes one of Impressionism's fundamental achievements. Not forgetting, of course, the freedom of treatment and the newness of the technique which were perfectly adapted to what they were trying to express. ☐

The last time Delacroix presented his works at the Salon was in 1859; in 1869 paintings by Monet, Sisley, Renoir, and Bazille were in their exhibition on the Champs-Elysées. Between these two dates, Courbet was ever present in the Salon, as were Corot, Daubigny, and Théodore Rousseau until his death in 1867, and Manet had been exhibiting there since 1861. These Salons were the "origins" of what would later be called "Impressionism," insofar as reference works for the young generation could be found next of Manet or Théodore Duret's *French Painters in 1867*. One of the Salon's prime advantages was that it gave painters the chance to exhibit. It was still an essential crossroads for the public (the interested viewers and the potential buyers) and the artists, especially new ones. Thus the question of who sat on the admission panel – dominated by the Institute until 1863, then by established artists – was regularly raised by the critics. The underlying political issue was, of course, freedom of expression. In 1859 Zacharie Astruc commented: "As long as exhibi-

Although seriously contested throughout the 1860s, the Salon nevertheless remained a reference for artists, at a time that witnessed the emergence of a "modern" school of criticism. By Antoinette Ehrard.

11

13

11. Castagnary preferred Daubigny's Vendanges en Bourgogne (Grape Harvest in Bourgogne, *oil on canvas, 67 3/4 x 115 3/4 in., 172 x 294 cm, 1863, Musée d'Orsay*) to his River Oise series: "What a truthful impression, what a sense of the French countryside."

12. After meeting Rousseau, Diaz painted landscapes in the Forest of Fontainebleau, *like* Les Hauteurs du Jean de Paris (The Heights of Le Jean de Paris, *oil on canvas, 33 1/8 x 41 3/4 in., 84 x 106 cm, 1867, Musée d'Orsay*), which were admired by Bazille and Renoir.

13. Constant Troyon earned a reputation as an animal painter in the 19th century: his Vue prise des hauteurs de Suresnes (View from the Heights of Suresnes, *oil on canvas, 71 3/8 x 104 3/8 in., 182 x 265 cm, 1856, the Louvre Museum*) is considered one of his most accomplished works.

to canvases by artists making their first appearance. The Salon was a state-organized exhibition of works of art and gave rise to an increasingly large number of critical reviews – no less than one hundred and eight in 1859. The authors did not simply appraise each work, one after the other (it would have been an impossible task: 4,240 entries in 1869). They made an evaluation and voiced their expectations. Among the dozens of critics writing at this time were a few who discerned the issues at stake during these decisive years – whatever conclusions they may have drawn. In addition to the reviews of the Salon, important articles were written on the independent exhibitions, such as Émile Zola's 1867 study tions are not free, as long as there is no ultimate recourse to public opinion [...], as long as no encouragement is given to young talent, we must despair of art in France." Zola provoked a scandal in 1866 with his virulent attack on the jury. The artists who took part in the first "Impressionist" exhibition, in 1874, were united by the desire to exhibit freely, rather than by a common aesthetic. Faced with an ensemble of extremely disparate works, the critics were often thrown into disarray. "Painting is sick, very sick. It has no force, little character, little strength," lamented Astruc in 1859. And Duret wrote: "The weakening of our school of painting is today [1867] an accomplished fact and unfortunately irreversible." He

12

14

went on to say: "All we can do is to cling to the works of the remaining masters." Which masters? In 1859 Astruc commented: "The vital sources of modern painting can be summed up thus: Delacroix, Corot, Courbet." He was seconded that year by Duranty who remarked that Delacroix was "the one young painters must fix their gaze on, not to copy, but to imitate his life history and to learn how to break loose from the common herd." In 1866 Jules Castagnary designated Fantin, Monet and Manet as Courbet's descendants, describing them as "the

realistic and idealistic youth" (which for him meant "Naturalist"). Two years later Zola saw Corot as "the doyen of the Naturalists, in spite of his predilection for mist effects," but he was unable to discern among the movement's younger members the one who would measure up to his predecessors: "I consult the future, and I wonder which figure will loom up large and humane enough to understand our civilization and to render it artistic by interpreting it with genius's masterly breadth." This anticipation of a future "genius" blunted the critics' powers of reflection, as did their constant preoccupation with the question of subject. Everyone recognized landscape's triumph, even if this acknowledgment was made with great reticence. "I will admit, like everyone else, that the modern school of land-

14. The critics reproached Corot for his clumsy execution of Souvenir de Mortefontaine (Souvenir of Mortefontaine, *oil on canvas, 25 5/8 x 35 in., 65 x 89 cm, 1864, the Louvre Museum). The blurred and mobile effects the artist sought in his brushwork were doubtless inspired by his collection of over 200 photos of landscape.*

15. In his comments on the 1863 Salon des Refusés, Castagnary praised the sketchlike quality, the force "the impression" produced by Jongkind in the Ruines du château de Rosemont (Ruins of the Château of Rosemont, *oil on canvas, 13 3/8 x 22 in., 34 x 56 cm, 1863, Musée d'Orsay).*

16. *This site inspired numerous artists from Delacroix to Monet. In* La Falaise d'Étretat, après l'orage *(The Cliff at Étretat, after the Storm,* oil on canvas, 52 3/8 x 63 3/4 in., 133 x 162 cm, 1869, Musée d'Orsay), *Courbet captures a fleeting aspect of landscape, which, in a golden light, balances the solid stability of the rocks and the movement of the clouds.*

16

THE SALON AND THE CRITICS

scapists is remarkably strong and clever; but in this minor genre's triumph and predominance, in this foolish cult of nature, unrefined and unexplained by the imagination, I see an obvious sign of a general debasement." Ten years after these lines were written by Baudelaire (1859), the hierarchy of genres disintegrated: "modern" subjects were held in the highest esteem. But it now proved crucial to repeat the revolution that had occurred in landscape in the representation of modern men and women. When Zola commended Monet in the 1868 *Salon* review, he congratulated him on never, to his mind, forgetting the human presence. One of the critics' major criteria in the 1860s was the search for men and women, as both subjects and actors in painting. It must be said that even those most favorable toward the innovators, when faced with judging the paintings at the Salon or elsewhere for their readers, used what was now a rather inadequate system of critical analysis. Which has nothing to do with taste. Zola wrote admiringly of Monet's *Camille*: "I caught sight of this young woman, trailing her dress and thrusting herself into the wall as if there were a hole." Further on, he said: "Look at the neighboring canvases and notice how dejected they seem beside this window opening onto nature." This desire to find "each figure in its place" in a painting, together with breathable air and a depth one can stroll in (Castagnary), was still relevant to early works by Monet, Pissarro, and Sisley. But it explains the difficulty the critics had when confronted with Manet's painting. Théophile Thoré remarked: "When one is a painter, one can do anything one wants." And Zola explained, in an imaginary dialogue with the artist about *Olympia*, in 1867 "You

needed light, bright patches, so you added a bouquet; you needed dark patches, so you put a negress and a cat in a corner. What does all that mean? You scarcely know, and neither do I. But, I know that you have succeeded admirably in painting a work of art, a work of a great painter." He continued: "I mean in conveying the truths of light and shade, the realities of objects and of creatures, in a lively manner and in a special language." There was no question of going beyond Naturalism. The notion of autonomous painting was unthinkable in the 1860s. Duret (who became the lucid defender of Manet and the Impressionists) was at first puzzled and saw Manet as "an artist whose principal shortcomings spring from the fact he started painting before he knew how to use a brush well." Should one conclude that there was a certain impoverishment of art criticism at the time of the birth of Impressionism? Not at all! "At every hour of the day, they express each individual transformation of the sea, this liquid sky, tempestuous, deep, infinite and as changeable as the one above. Effects of sunlight and mist, blasts of wind, pale early morning grayness, serene noontime brightness; evening's tranquil veiled mystery" – with Astruc's evocation of Delacroix's seascapes (1859), the elaboration of a literary counterpart to painting comes into play. When Duret wrote that the "glory" of a number of artists, "somewhat *impressionnés* [impressed] by the spectacle before their eyes," was to have "transmitted and communicated the exact tone of the *emotion* they were feeling," he went beyond the aesthetic of mimesis. "Impression" and "emotion" mingled in the critics' minds, but the stress was put on the former. In 1868, when Thoré mentioned Jongkind and contrasted "finish" with the painting of "impressions," he declared: "I have always upheld that true painters painted very quickly, and from *impressions*." Art criticism began to evolve into something more individual and sensitive when a group of writers dedicated their talents to an emerging "Impressionism" that nobody up to then had called by this name.   A.E.

17

17. James Tissot was a skillful portraitist of the rising middle classes: his Portrait de Mlle L.L., Jeune Femme en veste rouge (Portrait of Mlle L.L., Young Woman in a Red Jacket, *oil on canvas, 48 1/8 x 39 1/8 in., 124 x 99 cm, 1864,* Musée d'Orsay) is a fashionable and pleasant interpretation of a "modern" subject.

18. Portrait de Mme X..., La Dame au gant (Portrait of Mme X..., Woman with Glove, *oil on canvas, 89 3/4 x 64 3/8 in., 228 x 164 cm, 1869, Musée d'Orsay),* a large figure as elegant as Tissot's, was painted by Carolus-Duran on his return from a trip to Spain where he had admired the works of Velázquez.

FROM COURBET TO BAZILLE

The relationships between artists and intellectuals of all generations played a decisive role in the evolution of painting in the 1860s.
By Sophie Monneret.

Underlying the Impressionism that gradually evolved out of the successive trends labeled Realism, Naturalism, and the Batignolles school was a whole network of friendships, admiration, and antagonism. In one decade this conjuction of remarkable personalities led to the birth of the Impressionist movement. From Manet to Cézanne and Monet, from Baudelaire to Zola, artists and writers compared ideas and projects which gave rise to two lines of force: modernity and a pictorial technique well in tune with the constant agitation of the contemporary world. Pissarro's date of birth, 1830, made him

of their teachers: Couture, Picot, Gleyre, and so on, and the past or present masters they admired. Among the latter were three artists who fascinated them: Courbet, Realism's champion; Delacroix, with his magical play of reflected light; and Corot, the poet of the open air. They also looked in varying degrees to Guys, Daumier, Jongkind, Boudin, and the Barbizon school. Never had art gathered together as many adepts as in this second half of the 19th century. Murger's novel *Scenes from a Bohemian Life* proved a huge success among young readers and inspired many a vocation. Whether they arrived from the United States like Whistler, or

19

19. From 1860 onward, Degas' sketchbooks were filled with drawings of horse races, a subject that was to inspire him all his life; Sur le champ de courses (At the Racetrack, oil on canvas, 16 7/8 x 25 3/4 in., 43 x 65 cm, c. 1860-1862, Kunstmuseum, Basel) is an early example.

the doyen of the group which would later be known as the Impressionists. He was followed by Manet (1832) and Degas (1834), then by the much younger Cézanne and Sisley (1839), Monet (1840), and Renoir and Bazille (1841).
INFLUENCES AND CONTACTS
While learning their trade, they were subjected to the contradictory influences

from Le Havre like Monet, or from Montpellier like Bazille, they all rushed to the Closerie des Lilas café, breeding-ground for the Musettes and Mimis of Murger's novel, and to the bar in the rue des Martyrs where the second wave of Bohemians mingled with the apostles of Realism. "If that devilish Cézanne could come, we would rent a little room for two and lead

see page 26

20. Acquired by Napoléon III at the 1859 Salon, Jules Breton's Le Rappel des glaneuses (The Calling of the Gleaners, *oil on canvas, 35 3/8 x 69 1/4 in., 90 x 176 cm, 1859, Musée d'Orsay*) was hailed as a perfect example of Realism by a public that was often shocked by Courbet.

21. Millet's works evoked the taciturn sadness of 19th-century rustic life; *his* Femme faisant paître sa vache (Woman Pasturing her Cow, *oil on canvas, 28 3/4 x 36 3/8 in., 73 x 93 cm, Musée de Brou, Bourg-en-Bresse, France*), presented at the 1859 Salon, horrified Baudelaire with its "monotonous ugliness" and "philosophical pretension."

Following double page: 22. Despite its provocative sensuality, Courbet's La Femme au perroquet (Woman with a Parrot, *oil on canvas, 51 x 77 in., 129 x 195 cm, 1866, Metropolitan Museum of Art, New York*) was well received by the 1866 Salon public.

GUSTAVE COURBET 1819-1877
The painter of the renowned
A Burial in Ornans was one of
the outstanding figures of the 19th
century. Born in eastern France,
Gustave Courbet arrived in Paris
when he was barely 20 years old,
determined to be a famous artist.
Heir to Gros and Gericault and
schooled in the masters he studied
in the Louvre – Veronese, Titian,
Rembrandt, Velázquez, Zurbarán –
Courbet immediately established
himself as an innovator, who advo-
cated "realism" in painting. He was
soon to become the greatest artist
of his generation. Although he was
almost entirely self-taught and had
little conventional education, he
had great ambitions, and his art and
personality were more complex than
they seemed. Unfortunately, despite
being appreciated across the Rhine,
where his Romantic inclination was
detected, he was never truly understood in France, where he fascinated
and at the same time scandalized
his public. Disgraced under the
Second Republic because of his
republican and socialist opinions –
his friendship with Proudhon was
well-known – he set up in 1855
and in 1867 a one-man show,
independent of the Paris World's Fair.
His "Pavilion of Realism" revealed
the proud and bold temperament
that made him a moral and aesthetic
model for the next generation.
After 1871, although he had helped
save the Louvre from revolutionary
fury, he was held responsible for the
destruction of the Vendôme Column:
this unfair charge may have been
directed at the insolence of his
audacity and talent. This remarkable
artist spent the rest of his life
in exile in Switzerland where
he died embittered at 58. S.B.

From Courbet to Bazille

continued from page 22

a Bohemian life," Zola wrote to one of their mutual friends, on 29 December 1859. It would take Cézanne another year to obtain his father's permission to leave Aix-en-Provence. In Le Havre Monet's father had given in earlier and the young man was already frequenting studios (Troyon had recommended Couture's) and the Swiss Academy where Pissarro saw him in 1858. Degas, Manet, and Pissarro,

Manet's *The Absinthe Drinker* (Ny Carlsberg Glyptotek, Copenhagen) is a courageous fusion of Romanticism and Realism. His model was an ex-Bohemian turned ragman. Ever-increasing numbers of society's outcasts, so well described in Eugène Sue's novels, haunted the Paris that Haussmann had transformed into a vast construction site. Baudelaire wrote about them in his *Le Vin des chiffonniers*

23

23. *Camille Pissarro,* Le Chemin de halage (The Towpath, *oil on canvas, 32 1/4 x 42 1/2 in., 81.9 x 107 cm, Art Gallery and Museum, Glasgow). A preliminary study of this painting, which probably appeared at the 1864 Salon, can be found in Cambridge.*

the older members of the group, began to give evidence of their talent in 1859. In those years, Degas returned from a long stay in Naples, Rome, and Florence where, while at his cousins' the Bellellis, he began what would be his first masterpiece, the large Family *Portrait/The Bellelli Family (Orsay).* The same year, Pissarro exhibited at the Salon for the first time with a *Landscape at Montmorency* (now lost), but the entries of Fantin-Latour, Whistler, and Manet were refused.

(Ragmen's Wine); Manet most likely drew inspiration from this book, as he had been meeting the poet for years in the Divan Le Peletier. Six years earlier at this artistic-literary cenacle, which closed in January 1859, Jongkind had witnessed a discussion between Couture, defender of a Romanticism tinged with Realism, and Courbet, champion of an intransigent Realism, that was so violent a crowd gathered at the door and in the street outside. Couture gained his reputation with his

see page 30

24

25

26

CAMILLE PISSARRO 1830-1903
The eldest of this Impressionist
generation was already 25 when he
arrived in Paris from his native West
Indies. His father had just agreed
to let him follow his artistic vocation.
At the Swiss Academy he met Monet,
who introduced him to Renoir, Bazille,
and Sisley. Unlike his young fellow-
painters, Pissarro did not suffer
from adverse decisions by the
Salon jury and he regularly exhibited
there from 1864 onward. His rather
classical art, much influenced by
Corot and Courbet and reflecting
a serene temperament, was more
easily accepted at the Salon.
He preferred the tranquillity of the
country to the bustle of Parisian life
and settled in Pontoise, then later in
Louveciennes, where he could
transcribe on canvas the variations
of nature, season after season.
Joined for a time by Cézanne,
he had a profound influence on
this painter of the Montagne Sainte-
Victoire. He took part in Impressionist
exhibitions, after a stay in London
where he met Monet. From this time
onward, he would, in spite of himself,
become a kind of teacher; Mary
Cassatt and Gauguin, among others,
came to ask his advice, while Degas
was a regular visitor. Constantly open
to novelty, in the 1880s he adopted
the Divisionist technique of Signac
and Seurat. He would nevertheless
have to wait until his retrospective
organized by Durand-Ruel the following decade to receive public and
critical acclaim. He later returned
to Paris and undertook several major
series of urban landscapes, featuring
a limited number of motifs seen from
various viewpoints. After his death
in 1903, his son Ludovic sought to
gain more widespread acceptance
of this reserved artist's work. S.B.

Preceding page:
*24. After his success at
the 1859 Salon with* Les Bords
de l'Oise, île de Vaux *(The Banks
of the Oise, the Isle of Vaux,
oil on canvas, 35 3/8 x 71 5/8 in.,
90 x 182 cm, Musée des Beaux-
Arts, Bordeaux), Daubigny would
constantly be asked for more
paintings on this theme.*

*25. Like Huet and Daubigny
before him, Sisley chose
to depict the Forest of
La Celle-Saint-Cloud near Paris:*
Allée de châtaigniers à La Celle-
Saint-Cloud *(Avenue of Chestnut
Trees in La Celle-Saint-Cloud,
oil on canvas, 51 x 81 7/8 in.,
129 x 208 cm, 1865, Musée
du Petit Palais, Paris) is
one of the rare surviving
paintings from this period.*

*26. From 1866 to 1868,
Pissarro spent six months a year
at Pontoise; some of his finest
canvases, such as* La Côte de
Jallais *(Jallais Hill, oil on canvas,
39 1/4 x 45 1/2 in., 87 x 114 cm,
1867, Metropolitan Museum
of Art, New York), date from
this period.*

EDOUARD MANET 1832-1883
His contemporaries remember
the "blond Manet" as a brilliant,
charming, attractive, refined,
and cheerful man. He came from a
cultivated, upper middle-class family
and was a true Parisian – he hated
the country. Having abandoned his
idea of a naval career, he spent
almost six years in the studio of
Thomas Couture. But he completed
his training at the Louvre, studying
and copying masters like Titian,
Velázquez and Rembrandt. He was
resolutely anti-academic and was to
become the "painter of modern life"
Baudelaire wished for. Aware of his
talent and hoping to be seen as
a worthy successor to the great
masters, he struggled to gain both
official and critical recognition,
without modifying his style. After Zola,
the young generation acnowledged
him as a leader whose prestige
grew greater and greater: at the Café
Guerbois, people crowded around
this "color-bearer" of the new manner
of painting. After the various setbacks
he received at the Salon and the
uproar caused by *Le Déjeuner sur
l'herbe* and *Olympia*, he organized
his own one-man show, as Courbet
had done. Although he subsequently
grew closer to Monet, he did not
exhibit with the future Impressionists.
He remained fiercely independent,
appreciated only by a handful
of distinguished connoisseurs.
After Baudelaire, Zola, Astruc, and
Théophile Gautier, Mallarmé took
the artist's defence and later became
one of his closest friends. They had
much in common, both of them
being fond of cigars, fashion,
and pretty women like the painter
Berthe Morisot, his sister-in-law,
whom he often chose as his model.
He died at 51 without having
achieved public recognition. S.B.

*27. Eugène Boudin owed his
success to scenes like* La Plage
de Trouville (Beach at Trouville,
*oil on canvas, 10 1/4 x 18 7/8 in.,
26 x 48 cm, 1864,
Musée d'Orsay); they have
the vast skies of his pastels that
were so admired by Baudelaire.*

28. Manet worked on his Clair
de lune (Moonlight in Boulogne,
*oil on canvas, 32 1/4 x 39 3/4 in.,
82 x 101 cm, 1869, Musée
d'Orsay) from his hotel window,
producing a mysterious vision
of a group of women waiting for
the fishermen to return.*

continued from page 26
Romans in the Period of Decadence
(Orsay) and Manet was his student for six
years. They often argued with each other,
the teacher even advising his pupil to
go and found his own school. Although
Couture's style was a little limp, his mod-
ernistic qualities showed through when
he took his pupils to paint outdoors and
urged them not to use Raphael as an
example, but Titian, Rubens, and Velázquez,
to whom Manet and his friends would
make constant reference.
Their generation saw the triumph of
Realism that ended the long battle
between Ingres and Delacroix. Classicism
had become academic with William
Bouguereau and insipid with Paul
Baudry. The public delighted in rustic
scenes by Bonheur, Troyon, and Jules
Breton whose *The Calling of the Gleaners* was bought by the emperor and
was less subversive than Millet's *The
Gleaners* (Orsay), which the official Salon
critics had described in 1857 as the
"Parcae [Fates] of Pauperism."
Millet attracted a crowd of disciples to
Barbizon, where he had lived since 1849,
but his austere exaltation of rural life
proved wearisome. Realism's true star
was Courbet, with his "friends of nature"
who paid court to him at the Café Andler
or the Brasserie des Martyrs. In 1859
Fantin-Latour, Legros, and Whistler used
his friend Bonvin's studio to exhibit their
paintings that had been rejected by the
Salon. In 1861 the Realists organized a
banquet for Courbet to console him when
Napoléon III struck his name from the list
of artists to receive decorations, in spite
of his splendid *Stags Fighting* (Orsay). In
1861, his admirers – Fantin, Castagnary,
and the Stevenses – persuaded him to
open a studio offering an introduction to
Realism. He soon closed it, seeing as
"each artist's art comes from his own
inspiration." From his *A Burial in Ornans*
(Orsay) to his *Young Ladies on the Banks
of the Seine* (Petit Palais, Paris), with
his dense, sumptuous painting, his subjects
that were occasionally thought improper,
and his masterly sense of landscape,
Courbet dominated and ended an era in
which he had tried to prove that "the very
essence of historic art is contemporary."

THE MODERNISTS
In 1846 Baudelaire wrote: "Nobody listens to the wind that will blow tomorrow and yet we are surrounded and assailed by the heroism of modern life." In 1859 the poet wrote his most well-known apostrophe to modernity: "Modernity is the transitory, the fugitive, the contingent, the half of art whose other half is the eternal and the immutable." Instead of Courbet, Baudelaire chose illustrator Constantin Guys as his paragon, praising his unrivaled

l'herbe). Whistler settled in London, and his painting was a synthesis of his liking for Velázquez and the dreamlike realism of his Pre-Raphaelite friends. Manet had caught public attention shortly before with his exhibition at the Martinet Gallery, where his hispanicized works could be seen: *Lola de Valence* and *The Spanish Singer* (Metropolitan Museum of Art, New York). What is new however is both the brutality of the *Street Singer,* in which no colors blended into one

30

gift for capturing the moment. But Manet and then Monet embodied Baudelaire's reflections on the artist "of a striking originality in which what is left of barbarism and ingenuousness appears as a further proof of obedience to impression."
Baudelaire's "Painter of Modern Life," which foresaw the goals of painting during the next decades, was published in 1863, the year the Salon des Refusés projected Whistler into the limelight with *The White Girl* (National Gallery of Art, Washington) and Manet with *The Bath (Déjeuner sur*

another and halftones were suppressed, and his Tachist conception of *Music in the Tuileries,* inspired by Constantin Guys.
SCANDALOUS ERA
Manet's *Déjeuner sur l'herbe* was rejected by the official Salon for moral rather than aesthetic reasons. This scandal resulted in Realist painters like Tissot, Fantin-Latour, Legros, and Alfred Stevens, who were also friends of Degas and Whistler, forming a coterie around Manet, later known as the Group of 1863. The modernity of these painters lay more in their choice

29. 30. Lola de Valence *(oil on canvas, 48 3/8 x 36 1/4 in., 123 x 92 cm, 1862, Musée d'Orsay), the star of the Spanish ballet that performed at the Parisian Hippodrome, inspired the most hispanicized of all Manet's paintings and a quatrain by Baudelaire. She is found again in* Le Ballet espagnol (The Spanish Ballet, *oil on canvas, 24 x 35 3/8 in., 61 x 91 cm, 1862, The Phillips Collection, Washington), for which Manet had the troupe from Madrid pose in Stevens's studio.*

29

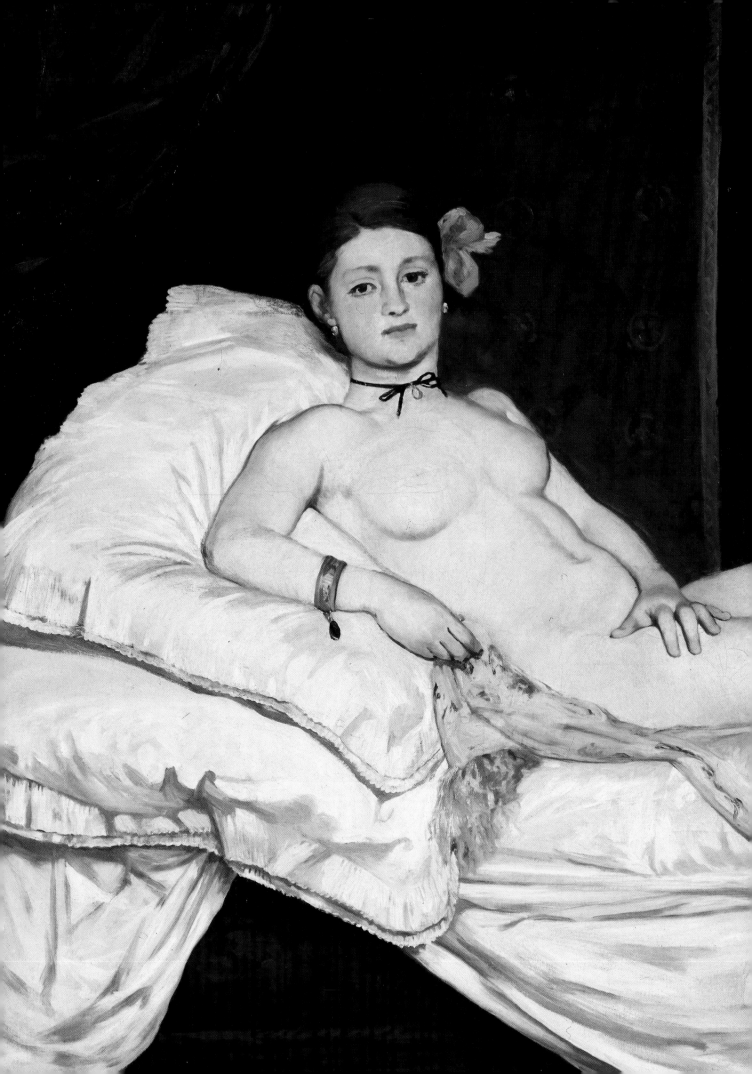

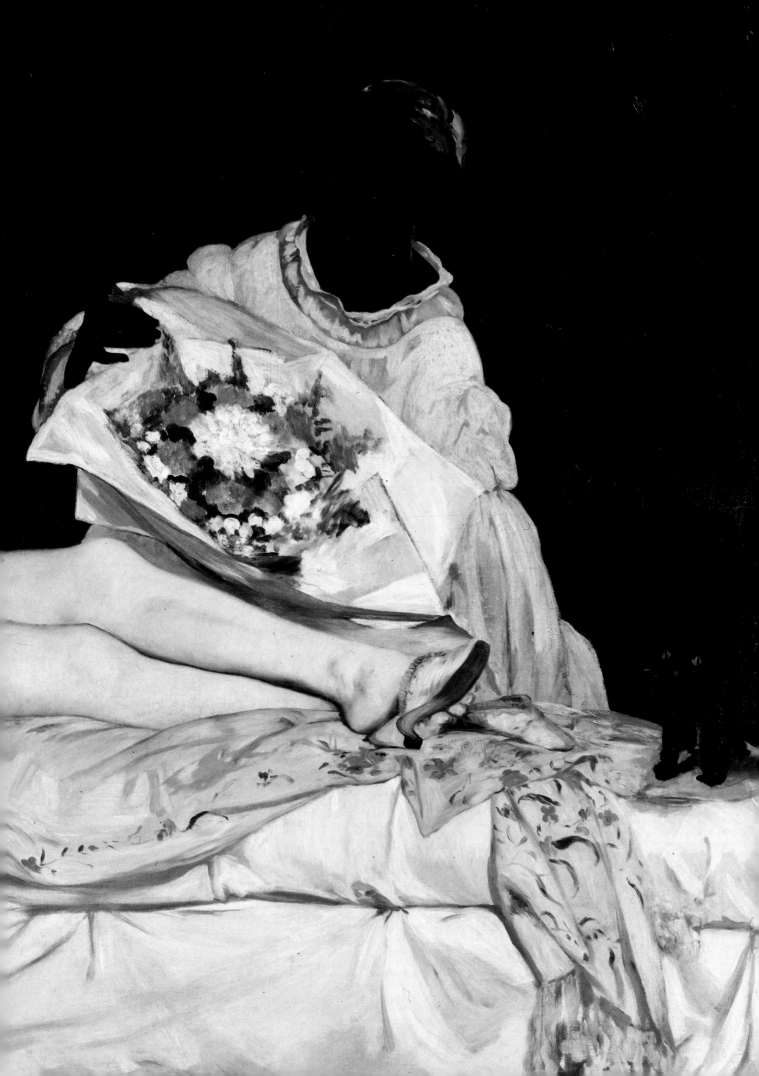

of subject than their technique, which remained faithful to that used by Ingres and Ricard in portraits. The uproar that greeted Manet's *Olympia* in 1865 gave him an even bigger audience. "Like a man falling over in the snow," Champfleury wrote to Baudelaire "Manet has made a hole in public opinion." Young admirers flocked to listen to his discussions with Degas and Duranty at the Café de Bade, meeting place for the empire's opponents, or at the Café Guerbois in the Batignolles quarter. In the 19th century cafés had great importance. They were a melting pot for people of different backgrounds, ages, and artistic and literary reputations; they were used as sounding boards, while the waiters acted as messengers: the waiters at Guerbois brought Manet and his friends the newspapers that wrote about them. No theory or aesthetic concept escaped scrutiny at these gatherings. Degas, Whistler, and the young Monet would talk heatedly of Japanism, for example. Photography was exhibited as an art form for the first time in 1859, only to be greeted by Baudelaire's diatribe. Its representatives at the Guerbois were Nadar and Carjat. Faced with growing competition from this new medium, pictorial imagination extended its scope into other fields. Champfleury wrote about the beauty of caricature and popular art forms (playing cards and earthenware depicting scenes of the Revolution) and explained Chevreul's discoveries and Delacroix's theory of reflected light. He was one of the ten admirers of Delacroix portrayed in Fantin-Latour's painting-manifesto *Homage to Delacroix*. Also depicted in this work are Whistler, Manet, who had asked his permission to copy *Dante and Virgil in Hell*, and, of course, Baudelaire. A year before the old Romantic's death, when consoling a pupil of his after a failure at the Salon, Delacroix confided: "I know from long and hard experience how impatient and sad such trials can make one." These words were spoken to Valernes, a close friend of Degas's. In his painting of *Jephthah's Daughter* (Smith College Museum of Art, Northampton), Degas borrowed the orangy-red from *Sardanapalus* that had so impressed visitors to the exhibition in the Martinet Gallery.

see page 41

EDGAR DEGAS 1834-1917
Originally called de Gas, Edgar Degas came from a bourgeois Parisian family, like Manet, who would become his friend and rival. But, though they were roughly the same age, their careers and temperaments were widely different. Degas was a pupil of the academic painter Lamothe who introduced him to the art of Ingres and Flandrin. He then spent three years with his father's family in Italy, studying the great Renaissance masters. His meeting there with Gustave Moreau proved to be decisive. Guided by Moreau, he studied Rubens, Delacroix, and Chassériau. Enriched by this eclectic culture, Degas evolved as both a classical and an innovative painter, developing an individual and long pondered style. Back in Paris, he was an active participant at the meetings in the Café Guerbois where his lively spirit attracted an attentive audience. Success was still unknown to him, as was scandal, and only a limited circle of art lovers were familiar with his work. As a "modern" painter, he was interested in the life of his contemporaries and was a regular visitor to the Opéra and to its backstage areas, to the racetracks and boulevard cafés. His eye was objective, rather than cruel, seeking the truth, the exactness of a gesture or expression. Despite his unshakable independence and his uncompromising attitude, toward himself even more than toward others, he took part in all the Impressionist exhibitions, from 1874 onward. But as the years went by, his difficult, irascible character, isolated him more and more. Nicknamed "Grizzly," he sometimes appeared bitter, in spite of the increasingly adulatory reviews he received. His discovery and enthusiastic practice of photography highlighted the last years of his life. S.B.

Preceding double page:
31. Manet's Olympia *(oil on canvas, 51 3/8 x 73 3/4 in., 130.5 x 190 cm, 1863, Musée d'Orsay) was inundated with sarcastic and even insulting criticism before being acclaimed; few other paintings in the world have caused the flow of so much ink.*

32. Edgar Degas painted the portrait of his friend the artist James Tissot *(oil on canvas, 39 3/8 x 44 in., 151 x 112 cm, 1867-68, Metropolitan Museum of Art, New York) who would make a career in London after 1871. On the studio wall behind him, a work by Cranach and a Japanese scene bear witness to the two young men's similar tastes.*

33. *Johanna Hiffernan, Whistler's mistress, was the model for* The White Girl: Symphony in White, No. 2 *(oil on canvas, 30 1/8 x 20 1/8 in., 76 x 51 cm, 1864, Tate Gallery, London), which met with great success at the 1865 Exhibition of the Royal Academy of Arts and about which Swinburne wrote a poem.*

34. *Degas first presented* Aux Courses en province *(At the Races in the Countryside, oil on canvas, 14 3/8 x 22 in., 36 x 56 cm, 1869, Museum of Fine Arts, Boston) as a family portrait; it is also a souvenir of a stay in Normandy with his friends the Valpinçons.*

35. Marine, Le Port de Lorient; *(The Harbor at Lorient, oil on canvas, 17 1/8 x 28 3/4 in., 43 x 72 cm, 1869, National Gallery of Art, Washington), a present from Berthe Morisot to Manet, still shows traces of Corot's influence; she and her sister Edma, who is on the right, had studied under him for several years.*

33

34

35

continued from page 37

Delacroix's influence can also be found in Degas's *Ballet of The Spring* (Brooklyn Museum, New York), as well as in his large historical canvases, *Young Spartan Girls Provoking Boys* (National Gallery, London) and *Scene of War in the Middle Ages*, in which strains of Ingres are also visible. The collector Valpinçon, a family friend, had

gave the poet the same attitude that he had made Degas take for a sketch in Rome. Their meeting in Italy helped Degas break away from what his father called "Flandrin and Lamothe's trivial limp drawing." Degas gained a better understanding of Delacroix and the Venetians through Moreau, whose sumptuous mythologi-

37

introduced him to Ingres, Classicism's stubborn champion, and Lamothe, his teacher at the Beaux-Arts, had instructed him in the theories of Ingres. These lessons are borne out in the purity of Degas's youthful drawings and his permanent dissatisfaction.

SYMBOLIST TENDENCIES

With the advent of Realism, the antagonism between Romanticism and Classicism became obsolete: they now merged into an idealism that was conventionalized by certain painters and ladened with symbols by Gustave Moreau and Puvis de Chavannes. In *Hesiod and the Muses* (Gustave Moreau Museum, Paris), Moreau

cal scenes are a pure feast of color. The subjects undertaken by Puvis de Chavannes – such as *Hunting, War, Resting* – were highly classical, but he was criticized for his simplified flat treatment and for his use of a naive Epinal style (like that evident in *The Fifer* by Manet, whom he may have influenced). This somewhat older artist had a very amicable relationship with Manet, Stevens, Degas, and Morisot, who often asked him for advice. Furthermore, his "preference for low skies, solitary plains… and bad weather that was livelier than fine weather" heralded the works of Sisley and Pissarro. Pissarro's

36. This fragment of a composition that decorated the Jas de Bouffan, La Madeleine *(Mary Magdalen, oil on canvas, 65 x 49 3/8 in., 165 x 124 cm, 1867, Musée d'Orsay), is a typical example of the baroque style of Cézanne's early works.*

37. Wagner was much admired by Manet and his circle of friends. "I had the pleasure of listening to the overture to "Tannhäuser" Cézanne wrote in 1868 (The Overture to "Tannhäuser," oil on canvas, 22 3/4 x 36 3/8 in., 57 x 92 cm, c. 1869-70, Hermitage Museum, St. Petersburg).

36

PAUL CÉZANNE 1839-1906
In 1862 the young Paul Cézanne left his hometown of Aix-en-Provence to join his childhood friend Émile Zola in Paris. After having studied at length the Caravaggesque works in the Granet Museum and Provençal landscapes, he spent his time at the Louvre and the Swiss Academy, where he met Pissarro, who was to become a lifelong friend. His early paintings express the ardor, energy, and violence of his temperament: his use of chiaroscuro and heavy impasto applied with wide brushstrokes recall Ribera's canvases. Only when he started working with Pissarro did his palette become lighter and did he acquire the composition technique involved in landscape painting. In Paris he could sometimes be found at the Café Guerbois, stamping ground for the artistic avant-garde, where he assumed a role of spectator rather than participant in the lively discussions. Shy and haunted by self-doubt, Cézanne's occasionally irritable character isolated him to some extent. He was a solitary figure who gradually moved away from Paris, unable to cope with his failure at the Salon and the critics' incomprehension. After a visit to Auvers-sur-Oise and to Pissarro in Pontoise, he preferred to stay in the south, near Aix-en-Provence. His long friendship with Zola ended in 1886, on the publication of L'Œuvre: Cézanne thought he recognized himself in the central character Claude Lantier, a kind of failed genius. Nevertheless, this anguished artist seemed to resolve his inner conflicts on canvas, and his works are one of the most masterly expressions of a timeless classicism on the threshold of modernity. He achieved his aim of creating "something solid like works of art in museums," even if his painting was not really understood until the beginning of this century, shortly before his death in 1906. S.B.

38. In this Portrait of Louis-Auguste Cézanne *(oil on canvas, 78 3/4 x 47 1/4 in., 200 x 120 cm, 1866, National Gallery of Art, Washington), a vague smile can be seen crossing Cézanne's father's lips as he reads the liberal daily newspaper in which Zola defended his son's friends.*

studies at the Beaux-Arts alongside Lehmann, one of Ingres's disciples, and Picot, a follower of David's, left him with an unremitting hatred of this classical school. It resounded in his conversations with Piette and was passed on to his young fellow-painters, Monet, Cézanne, and Guillaumin. His liberation from academic constraints was due to Corot. He met this landscapist either through one of his pupils, Chintreuil, or through Anton Melbye, brother of the Danish painter who encouraged him to make art his vocation and to leave the Caribbean for Paris. Corot's dancing nymphs, so well received by a public that had long ignored him, interested Pissarro less than his Italian studies into underlying geometry and his landscapes with disappearing roads. Their example, together with that of Chintreuil, Impressionism's undisputed forerunner, with his observation of atmospheric changes, led to Pissarro's admirable landscapes executed at Pontoise in 1867 (*Jallais Hill*). Almost all members of the Impressionist movement are in some way indebted to Corot; even Degas was fascinated by the way he treated figures and sometimes used the same sitter, the young Emma Dobigny.

THE YOUNGER GENERATION
The younger artists also looked to Corot. Thus the village of Marcoussis featured in *The Cart* was chosen by Cézanne as the site for his first plein-air landscapes in the region around Paris. Sisley followed in his footsteps in the woods at Louveciennes with his friend Prins, as did Lebourg and Guillemet along the Seine. Corot supervised the studies of the Morisot sisters at their studio in the rue Franklin and at Ville-d'Avray; in 1863 he sent them to Auvers-sur-Oise, not far from his friends Charles Daubigny and Honoré Daumier, to paint outdoors. Berthe Morisot would soon come under Manet's influence, but her small *Port of La Rochelle* (1869) stemmed from Corot's teachings, as did her skillful use of white nuances and the dreamy grace of her portraits. Auvers had been the center of what is today known as Pre-Impressionism since Daubigny had decided to live there. As early as 1859, he was one of Monet's favorite artists and

see page 47

38

39. *Painted by Monet at his aunt's villa,* La Terrasse à Sainte-Adresse *(The Terrace at Sainte-Adresse,* oil on canvas, 38 3/8 x 51 1/8 in., 98 x 130 cm, 1867, Metropolitan Museum of Art, New York) *is most likely the picture in dealer Latouche's window that, in 1869, according to Boudin "made the whole artistic community come running, while the forcefulness of this unexpected work brought zealous support from the young."*

39

continued from page 42

was the great initiator of the river land-scapes so characteristic of Impression-ism Manet would later copy his idea of sailing up and down the Seine and the Oise on his studio boat, the *Botin*; "He's the painter of a moment, of an im-pression," remarked Odilon Redon in *La Gironde* in 1868. The young generation he defended on the Salon juries discov-ered his dancing, fragmented brushwork. His style is however not as free as Boudin's and Jongkind's who, through Monet, presided over the birth of the new school. Boudin's cloud studies were as rapid as those of Turner or Constable. His delicate art and his brisk shorthand observation of fashionable beaches represented a new formula which Monet and Renoir would adapt to their own ends. "If I became a painter," acknowledged Monet, "I owe it to Boudin." Boudin showed Monet oil paint-ing techniques and the benefits of working in the open air; he took him to the Saint-Siméon farm at Honfleur, which attracted many seascape painters, and, beginning in 1859, introduced him to Parisian artis-tic circles. When Monet caught typhoid during his military service, he bought himself out of the army and went to Sainte-Adresse, where he met Jongkind and thus completed "the crucial training of his eye." The Dutchman was a regular visitor to the Normandy beaches and the banks of the Seine; in his work "every-thing lies in the impression," as Castagnary observed at the Salon des Refusés; in 1865 another critic praised "his art of total improvisation." Monet brought these two advocates of lightness (Boudin and Jongkind) to the attention of his friends at Gleyre's studio: Bazille and Sisley, who, like him, had arrived in 1862, and Renoir, who had enrolled the year before, ad-vised by Ouleway, formerly a student there with James Whistler.

Gleyre, a classicist and liberal Republican who painted watercolors with Bonington, never tried to thwart his students' incli-nations. In this he was unlike his former ·pupil Gérôme, the leader of the Neo-Greek movement, who painted meticulous archaeological reconstitutions and orien-talized scenes and who contested the New Painting throughout the 1860s.

see page 51

CLAUDE MONET 1840-1926
Claude Monet had his first success in Le Havre doing on-the-spot caricatures. He was convinced to devote himself to painting by Eugène Boudin, whom he met around 1858. On his arrival in Paris in 1859, he became acquainted with Pissarro, whom he saw again at the Swiss Academy. A few years later, after his military service in Algeria, he enrolled at Gleyre's studio, where he met Sisley, Bazille, and Renoir. He used to go out painting in the open air with the latter two artists at Chailly, in the Forest of Fontainebleau, and in Normandy. At this time he seemed to be the heir to Courbet and Manet, whom he met at the Café Guerbois. With his blend of Realism and modernity and his interest in all genres, he was the era's objective witness: railways, boat races on the Argenteuil basin, and the open-air dance halls along the Seine became the main subjects of his paintings. This was however a difficult period for Monet – even with his friend Bazille's generous help – for his family no longer provided any financial support. At the Salon his early success was followed by rejection, in spite of Daubigny, who was then the only one on the jury to defend the future Impressionists. The Franco-Prussian War (1870) forced him to take refuge in London with his wife Camille and his son Jean. There he met up again with Pissarro and Daubigny, who introduced him to the dealer Durand-Ruel. Four years later, the first exhibition of the Impressionist group opened in Nadar's former studio. Despite the critics' mockery and a period of misfortune, Monet gradually emerged as the leader of the move-ment and met with resounding success. It should be mentioned that the famous water lily series painted at Giverny entered the Orangerie Museum in Paris thanks to Clemenceau, one of the painter's undying supporters. S.B.

40. Twenty years after painting Mer et pluie *(Sea and Rain, oil on canvas, 20 1/8 x 28 7/8 in., 50.8 x 72.7 cm, 1865, The Uni-versity of Michigan Museum of Art, Ann Arbor), Whistler spoke of the importance of this work, which is part of a series executed at Trouville while he was staying with Courbet.*

41. La Pointe de la Hève à marée basse *(La Pointe de la Hève at Low Tide, oil on canvas, 35 1/2 x 59 1/4 in., 90 x 150 cm, 1865, Kimbell Art Museum, Fort Worth, Texas) was one of the two admission pieces Monet presented at the Salon for the first time; he was accepted and noticed "for his bold manner."*

40

41

FROM COURBET
TO BAZILLE

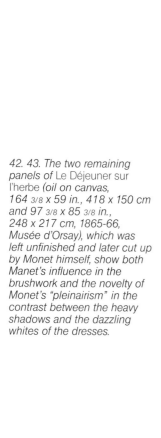

42. 43. The two remaining panels of Le Déjeuner sur l'herbe (oil on canvas, 164 3/8 x 59 in., 418 x 150 cm and 97 3/8 x 85 3/8 in., 248 x 217 cm, 1865-66, Musée d'Orsay), which was left unfinished and later cut up by Monet himself, show both Manet's influence in the brushwork and the novelty of Monet's "pleinairism" in the contrast between the heavy shadows and the dazzling whites of the dresses.

42

43

PIERRE-AUGUSTE RENOIR
1841-1919

Born in Limoges of modest origins,
Renoir began his career in Paris
decorating porcelain. He entered
Gleyre's studio in 1861 and met
Sisley, Bazille, and Monet, who took
him off to work at Chailly, in the
Forest of Fontainebleau, where they
were joined by the painter Diaz. But
his attention would soon focus on
the banks of the Seine, from Chatou
to Bougival. Accompanied by his
friend Claude Monet, he observed
the Sunday afternoon activities of
men and women, choosing as his
subject "La Grenouillère," a famous
open-air dance hall and favorite
bathing spot on the River Seine.
Working together was stimulating,
and the two of them would
engender what would later be
called "Impressionism." Unlike his
friends, with whom he set up the first
Impressionist exhibition, Renoir was
quite successful, thanks to publisher
Georges Charpentier whose society
gatherings he frequented from 1876
onward. His introduction into these
cultivated, bourgeois circles led to
several commissions for portraits
and décors. He went through periods
of endless self-questioning about
his art. His changing styles, often
interspersed with bouts of discour-
agement, can be seen in his "bitter
manner," where he conveys the
need to go back to a more classical
form of expression, notably through
drawing, followed by the "pearly
period," characterized by a return
to more pliant forms and the use
of a light palette dominated by whites.
However, he continued painting
up to his death, even when partial
paralysis set in. Success and official
recognition came to him during
the last years of his life, when his
canvases were inundated by the
sunlight of the south of France. S.B.

continued from page 47
BARBIZON

Gleyre's pupils inherited his taste for sunlit
countryside. When failing eyesight forced
him to stop teaching, his students fell
under the influence of the Barbizon school
and of Courbet and Manet. Bazille was
the go-between with the latter; he had
met Manet and Cézanne at his cousins
the LeJosnes. In the Forest of Fontainebleau, the huge Post-Romantic open-air
studio, they above all watched Théodore
Rousseau, who Sisley brought to mind in
his *Avenue of Chestnuts in La Celle-Saint-
Cloud* of 1867. Renoir drew so much of his
inspiration from Rousseau that dealers
could have signed his canvases with the
latter's name to sell them more quickly.
And it was at Chailly that Monet painted
his ambitious *Déjeuner sur l'herbe* which
was to mark a turning point in modern
art. After the sumptuous pleinairism of
Courbet's *Hunters' Lunch*, executed
in Frankfurt (Wallraf-Richartz Museum,
Cologne), Manet's Realism in *The Bath*
had been heightened by his addition of
a straightforward nude to this country
scene. Monet later proved it was possible
to pursue Realism even further, without
undressing anybody, and that zones of
sunlight and shade could initiate a revolution in plastic arts. His *Déjeuner* was not
shown at the Salon, but Monet had found
his direction. Courbet is depicted in the
canvas; he often went to see his young
friends, but though his influence is evident
in their use of the palette knife and in the
largeness of their figures – Renoir's *Lise*
(Essen), Monet's *Camille* (Bremen) and
Bazille's *La Toilette* – it was on the wane.
Courbet's friend the critic Castagnary
invented the word *Naturalist* to describe
this rising generation of painters, while
Zola coined the term *Actualist.* By defend-
ing Manet when he was refused at the
1866 Salon, Zola made a loud entry into
the world of art criticism. The intransigent
Salon jury was shocked by Zola's friend
Cézanne's baroque expressionism and rejected his entries. Cézanne's style revealed
his knowledge of El Greco's work which
must have reached him through Oller, a
Puerto Rican friend who had studied in
Spain. Cézanne's fellow Provençals played
an important role in his development in

see page 54

44

44. Frédéric Bazille Painting
"The Heron" *(oil on canvas,
41 3/8 x 29 in., 105 x 73 cm,
1867, Musée d'Orsay) was
painted by Renoir when the two
artists shared the same studio.*

51

From Courbet
to Bazille

45. Réunion autour d'un bateau
(Gathering around a boat,
oil on canvas, 20 x 24 in.,
50.8 x 60.9 cm, 1862,
Maxwell Cummings Collection,
Montreal), one of Renoir's
earliest known works, heralded
all his later preoccupations
with style and subject.

45

FREDERIC BAZILLE 1841-1870
The son of a rich banking family
in Montpellier, Frédéric Bazille
discovered Courbet and Delacroix's
works at the home of their friend and
neighbor, Alfred Bruyas, a famous
collector of contemporary paintings.
His frequent visits to the Fabre
Museum completed his preliminary
education and confirmed his early
decision to be a painter. Following
his father's advice, however
he began to study medicine and
arrived in Paris in 1862. He soon
left the medical faculty to enroll
at Charles Gleyre's studio,
where he made friends with Monet
and Renoir, with whom he went
painting in the open air at Chailly
in the Forest of Fontainebleau.
Though he let Monet persuade
him to accompany him to Honfleur,
following in the footsteps of
Jongkind and Boudin, he would
always prefer the southern light
to that of the Normandy coast.
In Paris, he met Courbet and Manet
(whom he admired), got on well with
Cézanne and Pissarro, and became
friends with Zola and Verlaine.
Better off than most of his friends,
he never refused to help them and
was remembered for his generosity
and his tall silhouette that can be
seen in *The Studio in the rue
La Condamine*. This promising artist
enlisted at the start of the Franco-
Prussian War and died on the
battlefield in 1870, before reaching
the age of thirty. He nevertheless
left us an ensemble of works of
extraordinary force and mastery. S.B.

46. After looking at Bazille's
La Vue du village (View of
the Village, *oil on canvas,
51 1/8 x 35 in., 130 x 89 cm,
1868, Fabre Museum,
Montpellier), Berthe Morisot
commented: "He is seeking
what we have so often sought,
to set a figure in the open air,
and this time he appears
to have succeeded."*

continued from page 51
the 1860s. Many parallels can be drawn
between his works and those of Daumier,
whom he probably met. *The Murder* (Orsay)
reuses the group from *Thieves and a
Donkey* (Orsay), while *Olympia*'s younger
sister curls up in the subdued pinks and
blues of Don Quixote; his use of glazed
flat tints in his portraits of Uncle Domini-
que is reminiscent of Monticelli who was
an occasional patron of the Café Guerbois.
Cézanne's violence was somewhat tamer
in *The Overture to "Tannhäuser,"* his
homage to Wagner whom the Impressionists all fiercely defended, while
the simplified draughtsmanship of *Paul
Alexis Reading to Zola* indicates that he
was also familiar with Japanese prints.
Renoir owed his lighter palette and fragmented brushwork to Monticelli and Diaz
who reestablished the link with the
long-ignored 18th-century manner. This
lightness is found in Monet's *Women in
the Garden* and Whistler's *Studio* (private
collection) and somehow rejects the
Realism dear to Courbet, their generous
companion of the previous autumn at
Trouville. This new trend was encouraged by Dr. La Caze's donation to the
Louvre and found an echo in verse form
with Verlaine's *Les Fêtes Galantes*.
Fantin-Latour's homage to Manet, *A Studio
in the Batignolles*, was a fitting end to
this decade with its web of interrelation-
ships. Bazille, who can be seen in the
foreground, would be killed a few months
later, but the sunlit strength of *The Terrace
at Méric* (Orsay) and *Summer Scene*
guaranteed his place among the masters
of the modernity for which he fought. The
epoch ended with Naturalism's triumph
and transformation. The painting of the
future is already visible in Renoir and
Monet's canvases executed during the
summer of 1869 at La Grenouillère. Not
far away, at Louveciennes, Pissarro and
Sisley's vision was also changing.
The era of major influences drew to a
close and Monet was the first to escape
them, as he said in his 1867 letter to
Bazille from Étretat: "One is too preoccupied by what one sees and hears in
Paris, however strong one may be, and
what I do here will at least be credited
with not resembling anyone." S. M.

46

47

48

Connaissance des Arts: The exhibition now on at the Metropolitan Museum of Art was mounted in collaboration with the Musée d'Orsay in Paris. As co-organizer with Henri Loyrette, you were specifically involved in the very large section dedicated to landscape painting.

Gary Tinterow: In fact we were both involved in the selection of paintings and their presentation, for each theme and each artist. As for the catalogue, we

in fact, was doomed. By 1866-7, it was dead. Landscape's rise to glory had been inevitable since the creation of the Rome prize for historical landscape, awarded for the first time in 1817, and since painters had become accustomed, from the 1820s onward, to executing preliminary studies, sketches, and drawings in the open air. Another frontier was crossed when Courbet adopted a new, more brutal treatment that left the handling of

A substantial part of the exhibition is devoted to landscape, which was one of the Impressionists' principal areas of research. In an interview with Sylvie Blin, American exhibition organizer Gary Tinterow recalls the different stages in the inevitable development of what was to become a major 19th-century genre.

49

obviously shared the work load, and I dealt with the section on landscape in two essays, entitled *The Realist Landscape* and *The Impressionist Landscape*. But most of the work was done jointly,

CdA: Landscape painting is one of the major themes of 19th-century art. With the Impressionist movement, it underwent an unprecedented evolution, especially in the 1870s. How was this genre viewed around the year 1860?

Gary Tinterow: It had been at the heart of pictorial creation for several years. As early as 1855, the Goncourt brothers had stressed its importance by pointing out that it was the only genre that interested all artists, to the extent of being compared with history painting, which official circles – the State, the directors of the Beaux-Arts, and the Academy – were still trying to promote. But history painting was now on the decline and,

the medium apparent. He nevertheless produced his paintings inside at his studio, as can be seen in his famous *Studio, Allegory of Painting* (Orsay). Théodore Rousseau was another innovator, albeit in a different style, through his use of more fluid brushwork, which was a complete break from the conventional smooth, overpolished painting. Official circles did not understand the "sketch-like," almost "unfinished" quality of his works. But the concern for realism in the choice of viewpoint and the importance of brushwork already existed.

CdA: The future Impressionists thus had "models" to follow.

Gary Tinterow: In some ways, yes. Boudin introduced Monet to working in the open air and Jongkind would suggest finishing the painting outside; Daubigny would be the first to do this in his search for "truth" and thus pushed

47. Following in the footsteps of the Barbizon painters, Monet chose to paint his first landscapes in the Forest of Fontainebleau; Le Pavé de Chailly dans la forêt de Fontainebleau *(Pavé de Chailly in the Fontainebleau Forest, oil on canvas, 38 1/4 x 51 3/8 in., 43 x 59 cm, 1865, Musée d'Orsay) still bears the traces of his elders' influence.*

48. In the 1860s both the Salon jury and the young generation regarded the elderly Camille Corot as one of landscape's great masters. Cour d'une maison de paysans aux environs de Paris *(Courtyard of a Farmhouse, in the Vicinity of Paris), oil on canvas, 18 1/4 x 22 in., 46 x 56 cm, c. 1865-70, Musée d'Orsay.*

49. Among the painters of the Barbizon school, Théodore Rousseau (Groupe de chênes dans les gorges d'Apremont [Oak Trees in the Gorge of Apremont], *oil on canvas, 25 x 39 1/8 in., 63 x 99 cm, 1852, Louvre) can be considered as one of the forerunners of Impressionism, to whom Monet and Sisley often went for advice.*

51

52

realism even further. Monet's approach would be even bolder: he tackled figure painting in the open air – a totally new genre – with his *Women in the Garden*. The mythical "plein air" experiment thus reached the completion stage.

CdA: What was he aiming to do exactly when he launched into this adventure?

Gary Tinterow: His goal was to be accepted at the Salon with figure paintings: painters could not yet win recognition or commissions from the middle-class clientele with landscape alone. Artists in the 1860s nursed the

CdA: So it was a time of great change and new vision.

Gary Tinterow: Exactly. It was a radically new, more realistic way of looking at things. In fact, painters wanted above all to give an "impression" of truth, and to have an impact on or even shock the public. They wanted to measure up to their elders too or even surpass them. The "new painting" thus resulted from the combined influences not only of Courbet and the Barbizon school, but also of Japanese art and the practice of working together. One could speak

53

Preceding double page:
50. Refused by the 1865 Salon jury, Monet's La Pie *(The Magpie, oil on canvas, 35 x 51 1/8 in., 89 x 130 cm, Musée d'Orsay) is one of his most ambitious landscapes: the off-center composition, the glimmering whites, the freedom of the brushwork, and even its title make it one of his boldest.*

51. Claude Monet frequently returned to the Normandy coast, which provided him with a wide variety of subjects: Le Phare de l'hospice *(The Lighthouse, oil on canvas, 21 1/4 x 31 3/8 in., 54 x 81 cm, 1864, Kunsthaus, Zurich) was one of his first attempts at capturing the fleeting quality of a particular moment.*

52. Immortalized by Renoir, La Grenouillère *(oil on canvas, 26 1/8 x 31 7/8 in., 66 x 81 cm, 1869, Nationalmuseum, Stockholm) was popular throughout the 1860s and attracted Parisians who wanted to bathe in the Seine.*

53. Sur la plage à Trouville *(On the Beach at Trouville, oil on canvas, 15 x 18 1/8 in., 38 x 46 cm, 1870, Musée Marmottan, Paris) illustrates Monet's desire to paint figures in the open air, while adopting a scene from modern life: bathing in the sea.*

Following double page:
54. Although they worked side by side, Monet's vision of La Grenouillère *(oil on canvas, 29 3/8 x 39 1/4 in., 75 x 100 cm, 1869, Metropolitan Museum of Art, New York) was quite different from Renoir's. Monet is more concerned here with the reflections of light on the water than with the figures.*

ambition of setting a figure in a landscape, or rather painting a figure in the open air. It was a genuine challenge as well, given the difficulty involved in such an exercise, which also enabled this theme to be linked to the notion of "modern life" at a time when history painting was dying out.

The large-scale works at the Salon would henceforth depict life-size figures instead of the battlescenes so often displayed before this period.

of rivalry and even a snowball effect: an idea used by one artist was often readopted by another. Research extended into all directions and landscape's evolution was no longer linear but multiform. Nobody could have foreseen that the Barbizon school would lead to *La Grenouillère*: the road was in no way laid out, far from it. That may explain some obvious backtracking, with, for example, Monet's 1868 *The Jetty of Le Havre in Bad Weather* (private coll.),

54

64

or with Bazille. A certain amount of hesitation and uncertainty still lingered, which convinced Monet that his *Grenouillères* were "bad rapid sketches" not to be submitted to the Salon. What are today regarded as Impressionist masterpieces were then often only unfinished experiments in their authors' eyes and cannot be considered as indicative of their intent.

CdA: Isn't that precisely what distin-

56

guishes them from the preceding generations? Painters from Corot to Rousseau frequently endowed their landscapes with a philosophical, moral or even sentimental purpose. How did artists like Monet, Renoir, and Pissarro tackle this theme?

Gary Tinterow: That evidently depends on the artist. But generally speaking, they weren't trying to deliver any particular message: in his observation of nature, the painter adopted an almost objective and neutral attitude. All that counted was form, color, composition, and brushwork: their unique message was the painting, which was sufficient in itself. The idea the canvas was to convey was inherent in its treatment and its very medium.

CdA: We have often associated Impressionism with landscape painting. Was this really the principal area of research of the generation of the 1860s? Did this upheaval occur through landscape?

55. 56. With Monet and Courbet, the sea and its changeable effects became a theme of painting. The former, in La Vague Verte *(The Green Wave, oil on canvas, 19 1/8 x 25 1/2 in., 49 x 65 cm, 1865, Metropolitan Museum of Art, New York), sought to render the impression of the sailing boats' speed on the huge mass of deep water, while in* La Trombe *(The Waterspout, oil on canvas, 17 1/8 x 26 1/8 in., 43 x 66 cm, 1865, Philadelphia Museum of Art), just by modifying his brushwork, Courbet conveyed the suddenness and the violence of the cloudburst on the seashore.*

Gary Tinterow: For certain painters, yes. For Manet, Degas, and even Renoir, no. Landscape wasn't their prime concern. For the others, it was just one of their many preoccupations. What was innovative, in fact, was the idea of abandoning, of totally rejecting the hierarchization of subjects, and even the subject of the canvas itself. As Henri Loyrette said, everything in the painting counted, the background was as important as the figure. The goal was to actually integrate the figure into the landscape.

CdA: This refusal to set up a hierarchy

riod were also "modern" in the way their subjects were inspired by their contemporaries' lifestyles. They were not the only ones of course: others had adopted modern subjects as well, but their treatment and style had remained very traditional. The artists whose works are displayed here stood out for their new manner of painting, notably for their insistence on the actual technique, on the painter's action and the medium itself, which are also a reality.

CdA: Few of their contemporaries really understood this new manner of painting.

57. Jeanne-Marguerite Lecadre au jardin (Jeanne-Marguerite Lecadre in the Garden, *oil on canvas, 31 1/2 x 39 in., 80 x 99 cm, Hermitage Museum, St. Petersburg) was painted during the summer of 1866 or 1867 in the grounds of Monet's friends the Lecadres' estate at Sainte-Adresse.*

58. Femmes au Jardin (Women in the Garden, *oil on canvas, 100 1/8 x 80 3/4 in., 255 x 205 cm, 1867, Musée d'Orsay) is one of Monet's earliest masterpieces; it no doubt depicts his companion Camille whom he asked to pose in different attitudes for this very ambitious composition, which was refused by the Salon jury.*

57

led to the breakdown of all the codes and the traditional classification of genres.

Gary Tinterow: Henceforth, a landscape and a portrait, a nude and a still life could be painted on the same canvas. Manet's *Le Déjeuner sur l'herbe* is a perfect example of this. What's it about? Is it a scene from everyday life? a landscape? a nude? In fact it's all these in one.

CdA: Hence the public's perplexity or occasional embarrassment at having effectively lost their points of reference.

Gary Tinterow: The artists of this pe-

Gary Tinterow: Certain people like Zola and Duranty did, or even Castagnary, who made an extremely lucid analysis of these young painters. He realized that this "new painting" was paving the way to the future.

CdA: Have any changes been made to the exhibition since it left Paris?

Gary Tinterow: No, there are no major modifications. The hanging policy has remained the same; we have kept the emphasis on the links between the various artists' works, exactly as in Paris. □

58

INTRODUCING NEW THEMES

By Marina
Ferretti-Bocquillon,
who collaborated
on the writing of the
exhibition catalogue.

HISTORY PAINTING

The 1860s witnessed Courbet's growing success and the emergence of new personalities, as the limelight faded for Ingres and Delacroix. Manet, keenly disputed but already famous, painted *Le Déjeuner sur l'herbe* and *Olympia* and thus assumed the role of leader of the school. The young painters who would later form the Impressionist group were still trying their hand at *"grande peinture,"* or the highest genres categories, including history painting. To escape these established hierarchies and conventions inspired by Italian painting, they turned toward other traditions and invented new solutions. With each successive work, a new, more lively, more rapid manner of painting evolved. By the end of the decade religious art had practically disappeared, history painting had merged into genre scenes, Venus was a naked studio model, and portraits often bore a resemblance to snapshots. Modern life was imposing itself everywhere.

LA GUERRE

59

59. La Guerre (War, oil on canvas, 43 1/8 x 58 3/4 in., 109.5 x 149.2 cm, 1867, Philadelphia Museum of Art) is a smaller version of Bellum, *the work presented at the 1861 Salon and acclaimed by the critics who saw Puvis de Chavannes as a young painter unwilling to make concessions to "the lesser tastes of the day."*

60. In front of Les Anges au tombeau du Christ (Le Christ mort aux anges) [The Dead Christ and the Angels, *oil on canvas, 70 3/8 x 59 in., 179.5 x 150 cm, 1864, Metropolitan Museum of Art, New York],* Courbet burst out laughing and asked Manet if he had ever seen any angels; Degas exclaimed: "There's a drawing in this "Christ with Angels"! And the paint is transparent. Ah! the old devil." Zola liked "these children with big blue wings who have such a gentle and elegant strangeness."*

In his critical review of the 1872 Salon, Castagnary declared that Realism had won the twenty-year-old battle against classical idealism: "We have all had enough of the Marys in the stable, the Samaritans at the well, the Magdalens in the desert, the hermits and penitents, and all the long procession of bloodied martyrs and emaciated saints. This biblical, allegorical, and mystical world is outmoded. It was less humane, less cheerful than the world of dryads, naiads, and nymphs, that charming deification of natural forces which sprang from Greece's bright genius, and it has aged more quickly. Let them both disappear; let's lock them up in history's storeroom alongside the castoffs of times gone by, and let the French Republic put the key carefully in its pocket." Realism's champion was right. During the 1860s history painting gradually exhausted itself, eventually vanishing, and was replaced by the direct observation of modern life. History, together with the Bible and Olympus, succumbed to the democratization and laicization of society. Its death finally put an end to the long lament over the disappearance of *grande peinture* that the critics had started in the 1850s and had continued throughout the Second Empire. This period witnessed a crisis in conventional representation and the emergence of a new manner of painting, which would not be called "Impressionist" until 1874. Ingres was in his eighties in the 1860s; he rarely painted and no longer exhibited at the Salon. But in 1863, the

60

V enus or Susanna, nymph or bacchante, allegory or odalisque… whether blond or brunette, but preferably with disheveled hair, they were the joy of art critics and cartoonists. In their smooth nakedness they vied with one another for attention on the Salon walls and aroused the interest of distinguished gentlemen who studied their comparative merits. Like history painting, the nude at the Salon was more often than not the insipid repetition of an outmoded convention. It was always just another version of Ingres's *The Spring* or *Venus Anadyomene,* with arm raised to show off the sinuous line running from foot to fingertip that emphasized the beauty of the hips and torso. The Venus that was to grace a middle-class apartment, whether reclining or standing, seen from the back or front, with seductive glance and taut white skin had a sort of standardized beauty. She could not offend the lady of the house's sensibility, as "the pink and black jewel" that smouldered under Lola de Valence's gaudy skirts would. The Salon Venuses had lost the force of Ingres's ideal, from which they stemmed, and had none of the fieriness of Delacroix's women, who were an expression of a phantasmic universe set in an improbable Orient.

However, while the most innovative painters gradually moved away from history and its pomp and ceremony, they still could not relinquish a subject that remained the touchstone of talent. If they hoped to rival their great predecessors, Rubens, Rembrandt, and the Venetians, they had to paint nudes. And when Degas painted a historical scene *(Young Spartan Girls* or *Scene of War in the Middle Ages)* it was probably because it enabled him to introduce the nudes that heralded his future works. To rid the theme of its historical connotations, artists resorted to simple "bathers" in a country setting. Like *Olympia,* the courtesan who bared herself without

pretence, the bathers unveiled their charms without taking refuge in a mythological or literary alibi. In a century marked by its search for truth, these more credible nudes gradually relegated the biblical Susanna and antique Venus to oblivion and served as a prelude to Degas's more realistic women washing and dressing. The nude was becoming laicized as well. At the 1853 Salon Courbet led the way with his rustic *Bathers,* in which a very

different kind of woman from a Venus emerging out of the waves or a wood nymph, displays her plump nakedness. In 1870, Renoir's first bather would be a barely disguised homage to Courbet's *Young Women on the Banks of the Seine* and *Bathers.* The young Renoir's *Bather with a Terrier* was also reminiscent of the Cnidian Venus, for he took a keen interest in ancient works. *In Young Boy with a Cat,* where the child playing

64. 65. Luxury, calm and delight… Inspired by Olympia, *Bazille's* La Toilette *(oil on canvas, 52 x 50 in., 132 x 127 cm, 1869-70, Musée Fabre, Montpellier) depicts a harem scene comparable with Delacroix's* Women of Algiers. *In* La Baigneuse au griffon *(Bather with a Terrier, oil on canvas, 72 1/2 x 45 1/4 in., 184 x 115 cm, 1870, Museu de Arte Assis Chateaubriand, São Paulo), Renoir pays homage to Courbet's* Bathers *and* Young Women on the Banks of the Seine: *his companion Lise posed nude for him in the open air; she can also be seen in a similar position on the right of Bazille's composition.*

65

64

with a cat follows Parmigianino's *Cupid Making His Bow,* he offers us a modern version of a classical model. Renoir was not the only one to adapt classical compositions. In 1859-61 Manet painted the superb *Surprised Nymph,* a direct descendant of ancient art, and in 1863 he presented *Le Déjeuner sur l'herbe,* an updated version of Giorgione's *Concert Champêtre.* Exhibited at the 1863 Salon des Refusés under the title *The Bath,* this work was singled out by unsympathetic critics, most of whom, however, acknowledged Manet's talent as a painter and colorist. Two years later, at the Salon, his *Olympia* provoked a much greater scandal. This time the critics were ruthless and overtly hostile to this painting of a prostitute on her bed. They forgot that Titian's Venuses were only Venetian courtesans. But Olympia's "indecency" was due to other causes: her body was neither beautiful nor ugly, she displayed it as it was; her gaze was emotionless; Olympia didn't act out of love or complicity, she was professional, and like Baudelaire's urbane characters, Olympia had lost the rustic innocence of Courbet's *Bathers* and so her presence at the Salon was all the more disconcerting. Courbet's *The Woman with a Parrot* was a direct response to the young Manet; when the painting was exhibited in 1866, the subject was immediately classed as a courtesan. But the painting's near-academic beauty gave *The Woman with a Parrot* "classic" status; even the most stubborn opponents of Courbet's art yielded with varying degrees of sincerity. Zola spoke of "going over to the enemy," but, in fact, the Master of Ornans no longer shocked the public. Manet was henceforth a leading figure for painters searching for something new. At the end of the decade, when the young Cézanne painted *A Modern Olympia* with such romantic impetuosity, and his *Idyll* with three clothed men and three nude women, the reference was explicit. However, Cézanne's interpretation was as passionate as Manet's was detached. He was directly involved in these erotic scenes, in which he openly depicted himself. Although Cézanne later renounced orgy and rape scenes, the

66. Cézanne's Pastorale *(*Idylle, *oil on canvas, 25 3/8 x 31 7/8 in., 65 x 81 cm, c.1870, Musée d'Orsay) is both his version of a pilgrimage to Cythera and an homage to Manet's* Déjeuner sur l'herbe.

66

nude remained one of his favorite subjects. But his men and women bathers,
having lost their carnal force, would be
treated with the same analytical detach-
ment as the trees above their heads or
the silhouette of the Montagne Sainte-

67

*67. 68. With his variation of a
classical theme in the* Nymphe
surprise (The Surprised Nymph,
*oil on canvas, 36 7/8 x 44 1/4 in.,
144.5 x 112.5 cm, 1861,
Museo Nacional de Bellas
Artes, Buenos Aires),
his Baudelaire-type* Olympia
and his Le Déjeuner sur l'herbe
(The Bath, *oil on canvas,
81 7/8 x 104 1/8 in., 208 x 264.5
cm, 1863, Musée d'Orsay),
Manet may be said to have
invented the modern nude.*

Victoire. Bazille paid homage to Olympia
in *La Toilette* where he adopted a theme
that Degas would soon make his own. A
sumptuous painting with classical tones,
La Toilette also recalls the harem scenes
dear to Delacroix and Ingres. Bazille was
above all an innovator in his reworking of
the male nude theme. It was no longer
feasible to paint a nude man as Adam,
St. Sebastian, or Apollo, so Bazille also
introduced simple bathers. The nude had
entered modern life.   M. F-B.

68

NEW THEMES
STILL LIFE

Throughout the first half of the 19th century, this "delightful" but minor genre was reserved for specialists who confined themselves to a favorite theme: dead birds, flowers, fruit, or precious stones. In Delacroix's works, still life appeared in 1848 – a fleeting phenomenon and a brilliant exercise in style. Courbet had tackled this genre in 1862, during a stay in Saintes, where he was stimulated by his host Étienne Baudry's interest in botany but would soon abandon it until his later imprisonment in Paris. Still life nevertheless became fashionable in the 1860s and

69. *One of Manet's early works,* Trophée de chasse (Hunting Trophy, *oil on canvas, 41 x 29 1/2 in., 104 x 75 cm, 1862, Musée d'Orsay), is a dazzling exercise in style.*

70. *Auguste Renoir,* Arums et plantes de serre (Arum Lilies and Greenhouse Plants, *oil on canvas, 51 1/8 x 37 3/4 in., 130 x 96 cm, 1864, Oskar Reinhart Foundation, Winterthur). The flowerpots in the greenhouse form an impromptu "bouquet."*

69

ceased to be considered as a negligible genre. Here again, the commercial success of a long-ignored genre may be partially explained by the emergence of a new clientele, who appreciated the celebration of domestic life and the straightforward view of a simple world. Its rising popularity was, in fact, due to several factors: the "confusion of genres" that upset the old hierarchy; the painters' sudden attraction to an art form which did not require expensive models; the renewed interest in the Northern schools and the rehabilitation of 18th-century painting, undertaken by the Goncourt brothers. Thanks to their studies, pub-

lished in the early 1860s, the long-forgotten Chardin was restored to his rightful place among the greatest painters. Changing taste was manifest in the success of works by Bonvin who, dubbed "the new Chardin," received the unprecedented, unanimous support of both official circles and Realist critics. Early still lifes by Manet, Monet, and Cézanne prove that the adepts of the New Painting were also sympathetic to this genre's unpretentious realism.

While it was no longer a specialist domain, still life nonetheless remained a test of virtuosity and an excellent apprenticeship for artists practicing "the difficult art of performing on canvas, the even more difficult art of holding one's interest with very little, with the painting's charm alone," as Castagnary remarked. In his *Grammaire des arts et du dessin* of 1867, the conservative theorist Charles Blanc pointed out that "the sole language inorganic life has is that of color... only through its color can a stone say: I am a sapphire, I am an emerald."

After the chiaroscuro and subdued harmonies of Bonvin, Ribot, and Vollon came a profusion of colorful bouquets that captured the savor of a particular moment: be it a token of love, affection, or gratitude, an ephemeral souvenir of a walk in the garden or the country, an armful of flowers. The goal of the New Painters thus slipped from one tradition into another, from Realist themes with working-class echoes – pieces of meat and loaves of bread – to a more decorative, middle-class register.

Toward 1870, the expression of the joys of living took precedence over that of toil and hardship. But in the years leading up to this period, the future Impressionists had tried their hand at the widest variety of themes: dazzling bouquets or hunting trophies recalling a stay in the country, works inspired by the elegantly restrained Spanish *bodegones,* by the tranquillity of the Dutch still lifes or by the opulent Flemish buffets; they reiterated Chardin's bourgeois integrity or adopted the more serious tone of vanity, evoking the fleetingness of time and the corruption that threatens all living things. Although

72

Courbet was receptive to the symbolic language of flowers, the floral paintings he exhibited at Saintes in 1863 were impregnated with a sense of nature. A student at Courbet's short-lived studio, Fantin-Latour also became an avid observer of nature. His subdued works, with even, Vermeer-type lighting, as in his poetic rendering of a table corner, brought him much success. Thanks to his friend the American painter Whistler, he soon made a career in England, building up a clientele who appreciated the somewhat repetitive charm of his compositions, often depicting a few flowers in a vase, or some fruit in a basket, a bowl or a plate, set against a neutral background. However, Fantin's works lacked the authority and the bold treatment of Manet, whose renderings of an elegant damasked tablecloth or of a peony stem weighed down by its huge flower were brilliant. From the still life of *Déjeuner sur l'herbe* to that in the foreground of the *Bar at the Folies Ber-*

gère, from the sumptuous composition in Washington's National Gallery to the simple bunch of asparagus of 1880, Manet long remained faithful to this genre which earned him the admiration of the severest critics. He even included still lifes in some of his most ambitious works. "Mr. Manet has portrayed both a balcony and a luncheon," Marius Chaumelin said at the 1869 Salon, acknowledging, "it is all painted by the hand of a master, with an accuracy of tone and a breadth of brushwork that is utterly extraordinary." The year before Odilon Redon regretted that Manet's *Portrait of Émile Zola* was "more of a still life than the expression of a human figure."

Monet immediately demonstrated his prowess in the art of still life and had similar tastes to those of Manet. Some of his early works include *Hunting Trophy* and *Piece of Meat,* which testify to his admiration for the works of Chardin, Troyon, and Ribot. *Spring Flowers* (Cleve-

71. 72. In 1864, Monet tackled a theme that would become his favorite motif: masses of colorful flowers in full bloom, of which Fleurs de printemps (Spring Flowers, *oil on canvas, 46 x 35 7/8 in., 116.8 x 91 cm, 1864, Cleveland Museum of Art) is a superb example. The same year, Manet executed his first flower paintings. They were devoted to peonies which the artist loved for their colorful blooms and decorative potential:* Un Vase de fleurs (Pivoines dans un vase) [Vase of Flowers (Vase of Peonies on Small Pedestal), *oil on canvas, 93 x 70 cm, 1864, Musée d'Orsay].*

71

land Museum) is a pivotal painting in the transition from Realist themes to water lilies, a subject that soon became Monet's favorite. That same year, 1864, when his friend Renoir painted the still life now in the Hamburg Museum, Monet

73 *P. Bazille. 67*

was still using Manet's frank tones and brushwork, but these would quickly be replaced by a more fluid technique and more pearly hues.

But Manet's still lifes clearly dominated the early attempts of these young Realist or Actualist painters. At the end of the decade, Cézanne's superb *Black Clock* was a homage to Manet, just as Bazille's *African Woman with Peonies* was a vision straight out of *Olympia*. This black woman's beauty adds a very attractive decorative dimension to this canvas, which is half-way between a still life and a genre scene. On the contrary, in Degas's *A Woman Seated beside a Vase of Flowers,* the portrait of his friend Mme Valpinçon, the still life is an accessory that helps to describe the model's character. Here, the mass of colored flowers in Mme Valpinçon's bouquet assumes a similar role to that of the very saleable works displayed in Tissot's studio which were intended to embody his personality.   M. F-B.

73. *Monet, Sisley, and Bazille* (Le Héron [The Heron], *oil on canvas, 39 3/8 x 27 1/8 in., 100 x 79 cm, 1867, Musée Fabre, Montpellier) were all attracted to the traditional hunting trophy theme.*
In 1867, while Sisley and Bazille were working alongside one other in a studio, Renoir decided to portray Bazille painting the heron (ill. 44).

74. *The solid structure of Manet's highly contrasted work* (Nature morte avec melon et pêches [Still Life with Melon and Peaches], *oil on canvas, 27 1/8 x 36 1/4 in., 69 x 92.2 cm, 1866 (?), National Gallery of Art, Washington) inspired the young Cézanne's* The Black Clock.

NEW THEMES
PORTRAITS AND LARGE FIGURES

Ingres's famous *Monsieur Bertin* would suffice to show that the portrait was a thriving 19th-century genre. From David to Courbet, there was no shortage of masterpieces and if, at the dawn of the Second Empire, some may have feared that photography would deal this genre its deathblow, they were quickly reassured. Overwhelmed by the number of bourgeois portraits cluttering the 1868 Salon walls, art critic Marius Chaumelin exclaimed: "Would to heaven that the picture cards had rid us of these awful portraits!" Unfortunately, there was still a battalion of them. Though Flandrin was acclaimed at the 1859 Salon with his *Young Girl with a Carnation* and in 1861 with *Portrait of Prince Napoléon,* these successes were rare. The increased quantity of conventional portraits, products of Flandrin's pale rivals or of Franz Xaver Winterhalter's frivolous followers, was deplored. Though this avalanche of works may have provided a number of painters with a livelihood, there were several who challenged established conventions. Works by Alfred Stevens or Carolus-Duran sought to express the physiognomy of the modern Parisian woman in the Second Empire. Even Courbet was attracted to this idea and in 1865 indulged himself by portraying the fashionable society that spent the summer at Trouville. Naturally, the adepts of the New Painting also attempted to update this genre in which they showed a passionate interest. "I am busy doing a portrait of my aunt and my two small cousins… I'm doing it as if I were doing a painting," wrote the young Degas to his father. As early as 1867, Castagnary noticed in Degas's portraits the "right feeling for nature and life." This was exactly the effect the suprisingly innovative artist was aiming at. His canvases were deliberately unconventional, as he pursued his search for the revealing attitude or the right facial expression or gaze. In *The Orchestra of the Opéra,* the portrait of his friend the bassoonist Désiré Dihau seemed like a modern-day version of a guild portrait. As a portraitist, Manet also used his family and close friends as sitters: the light-filled portrait of his blond wife Suzanne, called *Reading,* the portraits of his young pupils, Eva Gonzalès and Berthe Morisot, portraits of friends, art critics, and writers. But it was Victorine

75. Victorine undisguised. The light falls on the young woman's pale complexion which, like her red hair, is enhanced by Manet's "magnificent prune juice" color in the background (Portrait of Victorine Meurent, *oil on canvas, 16 7/8 x 17 1/4 in., 43 x 43 cm, 1862, Museum of Fine Arts, Boston).*

76. The merchant family from Le Havre, the Gaudiberts, were among Manet's earliest admirers. This commission recalls the typical Second Empire décor with its opulent fabrics and subtle elegant tones. The whole portrait has an air of good taste (Portrait of Madame Louis-Joachim Gaudibert, *oil on canvas, 85 3/8 x 54 1/2 in., 217 x 138.5 cm, 1868, Musée d'Orsay).*

Following page:
77. This portrait of Thérèse, the artist's sister, celebrates her engagement: the Bay of Naples is seen in the background as she stands showing the ring on her finger. Thérèse later reappeared in Degas's works as a placid expectant mother, then grief-stricken after the loss of her child, and finally as an embittered and prematurely aged woman (Portrait of Thérèse De Gas, *oil on canvas, 35 x 26 3/8 in., 89 x 67 cm, 1863, Musée d'Orsay).*

Meurent, the young model he met in 1862, who inspired most of his masterpieces from this period. He was charmed by the appearance of this pale, prematurelyhardened, eighteen-year-old Parisian, by her rather thin face and direct

75

but distant gaze. Victorine Meurent is the nude in *Déjeuner* and *Olympia,* and she also posed for a remarkable series of full-length figures, where she is seen disguised as a street singer, or as a matador, or as the bourgeois young lady dressed in pink satin of *Woman a Parrot.* These strange life-size figures, rapidly sketched or set against a neutral background, have been hung next to each other and are one of the exhibition's strongest features. In direct contrast with these fantasy figures painted in the manner of Velázquez, Manet's *Portrait of Émile Zola* was a "portrait-manifesto" or a public declaration of gratitude to the writer who defended the artist two years before. As in Degas's portraits, each accessory – inkpot, brochure, or print – has a specific significance. The newspaper read by Cézanne's father in his *Portrait of Louis-Auguste Cézanne Reading "L'Événement"* is a similar case. Cézanne deliberately showed his father reading the newspaper in which the artist's childhood friend, Émile Zola, published a vehement defence of the New Painting and the painter from Aix.

But the most explicit portait-manifesto remains Fantin-Latour's *Studio at the Batignolles,* presented at the 1870 Salon. In it Manet is seen painting the portrait of his friend the art critic Zacharie Astruc, surrounded by a group of young artists and writers. Three of them are watching the execution of the canvas: the German painter Scholderer who is standing a little farther away than the others; the young Renoir whose face is outlined in a golden frame; and the tall, thin Bazille. Behind the latter, stuck between the edge of the painting and the rest of the group, Monet tries to catch the spectator's eye. Fantin-Latour did not include himself in the work, indicating the distance he kept between his friends in the Batignolles group and himself. When Bazille introduced the same subjects in *The Studio in the rue La Condamine,* the more discreet portraits blend into a general view of the studio, into a modern genre scene. At this point, in fact, Renoir still looked like Manet's imitator and rival. The contrasted colors, relatively dry treatment, and measured

78

79

78.79. *During the 1860s Manet painted a brilliant series of full-length figures, rapidly sketched or set against a neutral background: from* Mlle V. en costume d'espada *(*Mlle V. in the Costume of an Espada, *oil on canvas, 65 x 30 1/4 in., 165.1 x 127.6 cm, 1862, Metropolitan Museum of Art, New York), which clearly testifies to his fondness for Spanish works, to* Fifre (The Fifer, *oil on canvas, 63 3/8 x 38 1/4 in., 161 x 97 cm, 1866, Musée d'Orsay), which is a homage to Velázquez.*

Following double page:
80. Le Cabaret de la Mère Antony (The Cabaret of Mère Antony, *oil on canvas, 76 3/4 x 51 5/8 in., 195 x 131 cm, 1866, Nationalmuseum, Stockholm): Mère Antony was the landlady of an inn at Marlotte much frequented by painters, including Renoir who depicted Sisley reading the newspaper* L'Evénement *in which Zola defended Manet and Monet.*

81. *Manet's* La Lecture (Reading, *oil on canvas, 23 7/8 x 29 in., 60.5 x 73.5 cm, 1865, reworked circa 1873-75, Musée d'Orsay) is one of the finest examples of the white monochromes fashionable in the 1860s.*

82. *Degas's art is summed up in his* L'Orchestre de l'Opéra; Portrait de Désiré Dihau (The Orchestra of the Opéra; Portrait of Désiré Dihau, *oil on canvas, 22 1/4 x 18 1/4 in., 56.5 x 46.2 cm, c. 1870, Musée d'Orsay) – it is a portrait of his bassoonist friend, a scene from modern life, and an early appearance of ballerinas on point in his work.*

80

81

composition of *The Cabaret of Mère Antony* – in which the daily newspaper *L'Evénement* is found once again on the white tablecloth – did not herald the silky mellowness, fluid brushwork, and pearly brightness that would soon distinguish Renoir's canvases from those of his Impressionist friends. Lise Tréhot, Renoir's young companion, played a role parallel to that of Manet's Victorine: she was the inspiration for *Lise with a Parasol,* "Camille's sister," as Zola and Astruc remarked, and for the anonymous figure in *Summertime. Study.* And the very modern portrait of the clown James Bollinger Mazurtreek was obviously closely related to *Mlle Victorine in the Costume of an Espada.* When Bazille tried his hand at portraits, he too used his willing friends and family as models. *The Family Reunion* (Musée d'Orsay) and *View of the Village* (Musée Fabre), featuring his cousin Thérèse des Hours, are fine examples of his talent for capturing both the stiffness of his middle-class, provincial family, who pose as if in front of a photographer, and the unaffected charm of his cousins in their light dresses. He no doubt remembered Monet's *Déjeuner sur l'herbe* for which he himself had posed in the summer of 1865, with Camille and Courbet who had come to Chailly especially for the occasion. Monet's ambitious composition, which was originally about 19 feet long and remained unfinished before eventually being cut up, was a direct challenge to Manet's *Déjeuner sur l'herbe.* It was also a prelude to Monet's *Women in the Garden* where, in a sunny garden, Camille, seen from the back, the front and in profile, poses in a white dress. All the essence of Impressionism is here: in the harmonious relationship between the figures and nature, in the scene's lively play of light and shade, in the bright colors and vivacious brushwork. But above all, Impressionism is found in the apparent simplicity which proclaims, as Stendhal did, that beauty is merely a promise of happiness.   M. F-B.

82

NEW THEMES
MODERN LIFE

*B*eauty, fashion, and happiness – this was the title Baudelaire gave to the first chapter of his study on the painter of modern life. From the early 1860s he incited the modern artist to capture "the special beauty, the beauty of circumstance and traits of character." He went on to say that "in the everyday meta-morphosis of outside elements there is a rapidity of movement that compels the artist to work with an equal speed." According to Zola, a canvas should soon "make a hole in the wall," while Jules Vallès urged painters "to look at life," failing which they would arouse boredom or indifference. From the beginning of the 1860s onward, contemporary life was in vogue: painters and writers carefully observed the changes taking place in their epoch. And it is true that the spectacle before their eyes deserved their attention. Under Haussmann's guidance, Paris was being transformed into a modern city, with wide boulevards, light-colored buildings, parks, and gardens. Among the crowds that thronged to these new public areas were the elegant ladies who carried delicate parasols and whose pale silhouettes in full crinoline skirts stood out against the dark-suited dandies and strollers intent on being fashionable. This modern Paris reflected the dynamism of a society in the process of industrialization, which had adopted capitalism and was organizing its leisure time and displaying its wealth at Universal Exhibitions. People enjoyed fashion and going to dances, the opera, and the theater. Race meetings and water sports became popular – England was very much in vogue – and there was a flurry of construction – such as the laying out of the Bois de Boulogne, the building of the new Opéra, the development of the railway, and the creation of Deauville.

The future Impressionists observed the transformation of their universe with growing enthusiasm. With each successive work, they adapted their technique to the expression of a fugitive, changeable beauty and painted its most attractive aspects with obvious pleasure. Unlike those of their elders – Daumier, Millet, or Courbet – their canvases ignored the

83. Going to the horse races was popular in Paris or near the Normandy beaches. Degas revived the genre scene with Le Défilé; Chevaux de course devant les tribunes *(The Parade; Horses before the Stands, peinture à l'essence on paper mounted on canvas, 18 1/8 x 24 in., 46 x 61 cm, c. 1866-68, Musée d'Orsay).*

darker sides of an era that combined profit, pleasure, and leisure with apparent ease. The adepts of the New Painting did not touch on their own personal difficulties, failures, disappointments, or financial problems. Only Degas indicated the more disturbing aspects of bourgeois intimacy in *Interior (The Rape)* or in *Sulking,* an evocation of the tensions that exist between an ill-matched couple. But it was the pleasures of the days, the details and characteristic attitudes of the times that preoccupied most artists. The future Impressionists were not the only ones to

But clearly, from the early 1860s onward, the innovators were no longer concerned with eternity or the ideal of beauty. These painters now sought a fugitive reality, ever-moving and transient, like modern life. As an observer strolling through the streets of Paris, the artist, the "sensitive and passionate daguerreotype," records the spectacle before his eyes, like a photographic plate, with no moral or philosophical intent. The rapid evolution of the studio theme was indicative of this trend. While Courbet endowed it with the "real allegory" dimension and thus raised it to

85

take an interest in this emergent modernity. When Baudelaire wished for "a painter of modern life," he had Constantin Guys in mind. Two years later, Théophile Gautier made this comment about Alfred Stevens, who was the first artist to pursue the idea of depicting the Second Empire woman: "He doesn't go very far to find his subjects and his painting is all the better for it." Today, Guys's gracious tone and Stevens's middle-class sentimentalism are too outdated to arouse any real enthusiasm. Apart from their choice of modern subject, they seem conventional or complacent. Like Tissot or Toulmouche, they are viewed with amused curiosity or with annoyance at the use of a real skill to produce just charming, seductive effects.

the rank of history painting, Fantin-Latour treated his *Studio at the Batignolles* with the solemnity of a group portrait, of a conversation piece in modern dress. Bazille's studio is a simple evocation of an informal, friendly gathering, a genre scene. But, despite this apparent insignificance, the subject being discussed in this studio is painting and the canvases on the walls, all of which are identifiable, play a real role. Outside the studio, Paris was changing, with its cafés, shows, and varied population which, from the dandy in the Tuileries Gardens to the singer in the streets, liked to be seen. Manet pays these Parisians homage in *Music in the Tuileries;* they were also depicted in the gazettes of the day. For the painters that

84. In 1874 Edgar Degas brought Edmond de Goncourt to his studio. "He showed us his foreshortened washerwomen in their graceful poses... and spoke their language explaining to us the technique of pressing and circular ironing, etc." (La Repasseuse [A Woman Ironing], *oil on canvas, 36 1/4 x 29 1/3 in., 92.5 x 74 cm, 1869, Neue Pinakothek, Munich).*

85. "My genre scene painting" is how Degas described his Intérieur (Le Viol) (Interior [The Rape], *oil on canvas, 32 x 45 in., 81 x 116 cm, c. 1868-69, Museum of Art, Philadelphia). The scene is indeed far removed from the epic rapes of classical painting. Here the artist views social and sexual inequality without pathos or complacency.*

84

Zola, for want of something better, called "Actualists" drew their inspiration from the same sources as the illustrators of La *Vie parisienne, Paris-Caprice,* or *Journal amusant.* Boatsmen and boatswomen, laundresses and soldiers, and cocottes – "charming animals that live everywhere and die in the hospital" – were targeted by the caricaturists whose favorite themes included fashion, society balls, shows, horse races, and open-air dance halls. On the weekend Parisians left the town to go to the country, with a marked prefer-

Salon. Together with Renoir, he undertook a series of studies in which he analyzed the reflection of the sky and the leaves on the water. With brisk, lively brush-strokes, he jotted down the figures of the regular visitors. The painting for the Salon was never executed, but thirty years later these brilliant jottings would seem like the very definition of Impressionism. Bazille, with his vast *Summer Scene* depicting young men in swimming costumes, was accepted and acclaimed at the Salon. Thanks to the rapidly expanding western railway, the Normandy coast became easily accessible to homesick or nature-loving Parisians. They would watch the transatlantic liners leave the port of Le Havre for the ten-day crossing to New York. They would head for the beaches of Sainte-Adresse, Trouville, or Hon-

86

ence for the banks of the Seine. Among the numerous establishments ready to welcome them was the famous La Grenouillère. Located on the Isle of Croissy, opposite Bougival, it became increasingly successful during the 1860s. Two barges moored to the bank and equipped with covered terrace offered a wide range of fashionable entertainment: swimming and boating, watching regattas, dining and dancing, all in a very free atmosphere. This popular modern Cythera attracted a motley clientele. Women wore bathing costumes or men's suits and smoked pipes. Boatsmen and *"grenouilles"* (women of easy virtue who did not necessarily sell their favors), artists and journalists rubbed shoulders with a more elegant society: it was Prince Bibesco who introduced Renoir to La Grenouillère. In 1869 it had such a reputation that the emperor and empress made a brief visit. That same year Monet decided to paint a canvas of this establishment for the

fleur. Monet, who had grown up in Le Havre, observed the metamorphosis of these places now given over to leisure-time activities. *Terrace at Sainte-Adresse* depicts a small group of holiday makers facing the sea on which sailing boats and steamships weave about. The tourists add the liveliest notes: parasols and panamas, flags flapping in the wind, and beds of gladioli capture the dazzling Normandy light. In Trouville Manet painted *L'Hôtel des Roches Noires,* the "king of the Normandy coast" that offered one hundred and fifty rooms to visitors. In Boulogne Manet sketched a landscape full of horizontals and transparent colors. Here again, the holiday makers' scattered silhouettes set the tone. Spread out across this pale decor like the notes on a musician's score, they create a me-lodious, airy composition; the parasols and light dresses provide the rhythm and alternate with the dark hats and children in navy blue suits.   M. F-B.

86. Fluid brushwork, transparent tones, a briskly sketched evoca-tion of leisure. With his Sur la plage de Boulogne *(On the Beach at Boulogne, oil on canvas, 12 3/4 x 26 in., 32.4 x 66 cm, 1868, Virginia Museum of Fine Arts, Richmond), Manet became an Impressionist.*

87. Energy, speed, and transience are captured in the Courses à Longchamp *(Races at Longchamp, oil on canvas, 17 1/4 x 33 1/4 in., 43.9 x 84.5 cm, 1867 (?), Art Institute, Chicago) by Manet.*

88. In 1862, La Musique aux Tuileries *(Music in the Tuileries, oil on canvas, 30 x 46 1/2 in., 76.2 x 118 cm, 1862, The Trustees of the National Gallery, London), one of fashionable Parisian society's minor events, made Manet the true painter of modern life.*

87

88

94

CHRONOLOGY

1855 Opening of the Universal Exhibition in Paris: Courbet organizes his own one-man show in his Pavilion of Realism.
1856 Duranty founds the review *Réalisme.*
1857 Baudelaire publishes *Les Fleurs du mal (The Flowers of Evil)*. Pissarro works at the Swiss Academy.
1858 At Le Havre Monet meets Boudin, who invites him to work in the open air
1859 Napoléon III grants amnesty to the political prisoners of 1851. Baudelaire writes his last review of the Salon, which admits photographers for the first time. Foundation of the *Gazette des Beaux-Arts*; French victories over the Austrians at Magenta and Solferino.
1860 Paris is enlarged and divided into 20 arrondissements. The renovation program launched by Haussmann changed the capital permanently. Nice and Savoy annexed to France.
1861 Ingres completes *Le Bain Turc (The Turkish Bath)*. Puvis de Chavannes presents *Concordia* and *Bellum* at the Salon. Mexico is occupied by French, English, and Spanish troops.
1862 Europe discovers Japanese art at the Universal Exhibition in London. Monet, Renoir, Sisley, and Bazille work together in Gleyre's studio.
1863 Thousands of primary schools created by Duruy. French vineyards are decimated by phylloxera. Napoléon III buys Cabanel's *La Naissance de Vénus (The Birth of Venus)* and authorizes the opening of the Salon des Refusés where among the works displayed is Manet's scandalous *Déjeuner sur l'herbe*. Death of Delacroix.
1864 Creation of the First International in London. Workers granted the right to strike by Napoléon.
1865 Chevreul publishes *Des couleurs et leurs applications aux arts industriels à l'aide du cercle chromatique*. Manet's *Olympia* causes an uproar at the Salon. Zola publishes his first work, *Confession de Claude*, dedicated to Cézanne.
1866 Manet and Renoir are rejected by the Salon jury. They meet Monet, Degas, and Bazille regularly at the Café Guerbois.
1867 Opening of the Universal Exhibition in Paris. As in 1855, Courbet opens his own pavilion. Death of Ingres and of Baudelaire. Karl Marx publishes the first volume of his *Das Kapital*. Renoir, Sisley,

Bazille, and Monet sign a petition demanding the opening of another Salon des Refusés. Charles Blanc publishes his *Grammaire des arts et du dessin*. Maximilian is executed by a firing squad in Mexico.
1868 The freedom of the press and the partial right to hold public meetings are not enough to calm political opposition and workers' and peasants' uprisings against the Empire. Napoléon III orders the dissolution of the International. Opening of Labrouste's Bibliothèque Nationale (National Library).
1869 Opening of the Suez Canal. Monet's *La Pie (The Magpie)* and *Femmes au jardin*

89. History painting enters the domain of current events: Manet's L'Exécution de Maximilien (The Execution of Maximilian, oil on canvas, 99 1/4 x 120 in., 252 x 305 cm, 1868-69, Städische Kunsthalle, Mannheim).

90. Nadar's own photograph of his former studio, on the boulevard des Capucines in Paris: this is where the first Impressionist exhibition was held in 1874.

(Women in the Garden) refused by the Salon. Together with Renoir, he adopts a new subject: La Grenouillère, the open-air dance hall on the Seine, near Bougival.
1870 Naploéon III remains in power after a plebiscite, despite the opposition's calls for a parliamentary regime. The war with Prussia ends with France's defeat at Sedan, and the proclamation, two days later, of the 3rd Republic. France surrenders Alsace and Lorraine. While in exile in London, Monet meets the dealer Durand-Ruel.
1871 The fall of Paris. The Commune ends in bloodshed. Courbet is unfairly convicted for the destruction of the Vendôme Column.
1872 Monet paints *Impression, soleil levant (Impression, Sunrise)*.
1874 First Impressionist exhibition is held in Nadar's former studio.   S.B.

89

90

PRACTICAL INFORMATION

Origins of Impressionism - September 27, 1994-January 8, 1995
The Metropolitan Museum of Art: The Tisch Galleries and Iris and B. Gerald Cantor
Exhibition Hall, second floor. 1000 Fifth Av., New York NY 10028-0198
Recorded Information: (212) 535 7710 - Museum Switchboard: (212) 879 5500.
Opening hours: Sunday, Tuesday, Wednesday, Thursday 9.30 am to 5.15 pm;
Friday, Saturday 9.30 am to 8.45 pm; closed mondays.
Catalogue written by Gary Tinterow and Henri Loyrette, distributed by Harry N. Abrams, Inc.
(502 pages, 620 illustrations, 220 in full color $60 for hardcover, $45 for the paperback).
In conjunction with the exhibition, The Metropolitan Museum of Art will be offering a
number of educational programs. At least four lectures will be offered, free with admission.
A number of documentary films on the artists represented in the exhibition will be
screened, and there will be special programs for teachers, a limited number
of guided school tours, family programs, and a printed guide for families.
The Exhibition is sponsored by Philip Morris Companies Inc.

91

91. Édouard Manet,
Mme Manet au piano (Mme
Manet at the Piano, *oil on can-*
vas, 15 x 18 1/4 in., 38 x 46 cm,
1867-68, Musée d'Orsay).

92. Édouard Manet, Sur la plage
de Boulogne (On the Beach
at Boulogne, *oil on canvas,*
12 3/4 x 26 in., 32 x 66 cm,
1868, Virginia Museum of Fine
Arts, Richmond).

Back cover:

Auguste Renoir, Arums et
plantes de serre (Arum Lilies
and Greenhouse Plants, *oil on*
canvas, 130 x 96 cm, 1864,
Oskar Reinhart Foundation,
Winterthur).

CONNAISSANCE DES ARTS - Numéro hors série. **REDACTEUR EN CHEF:** Philip JODIDIO. - **DIRECTION ARTISTIQUE:**
Sylvie CHESNAY. **DIRECTION HORS SERIE:** Virginie de LA BATUT. **CONCEPTION DE CE NUMERO:** Sylvie BLIN. **P.A.O.:**
Bruno HERVIEUX. **SECRETARIAT DE REDACTION:** Françoise FOULON, Claire MULKAI. **SERVICE PHOTOS:** Martine
JOSSE. **SECRETARIAT:** Inès DUVAL, Monique FOUQUET, Kathryn LEVESQUE. **ONT COLLABORE A CE NUMERO:**
Antoinette Ehrard, Marina Ferretti-Bocquillon, Henri Loyrette, Sophie Monneret, Gary Tinterow. **TRADUCTION:** Pamela
HARGREAVES. **DIRECTEUR TECHNIQUE:** Christian LECOCQ. **SERVICE COMMERCIAL:** Philippe THOMAS.

CREDITS PHOTOS: Couverture et Pages: 11, 26, 27 ht, 33, 38, 39 ht, 44-5, 60, 61, 70 bas, 76, 88 ht: photos des musées.
Pages: 2, 94, 99: Ron Jennings. Pages: 4, 5, 8-9, 12, 13, 14, 15, 16, 17, 18-9, 20, 21, 23 ht, 31, 32, 34-5, 40, 48, 49, 50, 56, 57,
58-9, 67, 70 ht, 71, 74-5, 77, 78, 81, 85, 86, 87 bas, 88 bas, 89, 90-1, 98: R.M.N. Pages: 7 ht, 41, 66: Scala. Pages: 7 bas, 23
bas: Lauros-Giraudon. Page 10: President & Fellows Harvard College, Harvard University Art Museum. Page 22: Hinz/Basel.
Pages: 24, 62-3, 64, 69, 87 ht: Bequest of Mrs H.O. Havemeyer. The H.O. Havemeyer Collections. Pages: 25, 30, 37, 47, 51,
54, 97: Bibliothèque Nationale, Paris. Page 27 bas: Bulloz. Page 28: Bequest of William Church Osborn. Pages: 29, 42:
archives Skira. Page 36: Roger Fund. Page 39 bas: Ailsa Mellon Bruce Coll. Page 43: Paul Mellon Coll. Page 46 ht: Bequest
of Margaret Watson Parker; bas: Michael Bodycomb. Pages: 52-3, 96: D.R. Pages: 55, 72, 82: Frédéric Jaulmes. Pages: 65,
68: The John G. Johnson Coll. Pages 73, 94 bas: Bridgeman Art Library/Edimédia. Page 79: Jochen Remmer/Artothek.
Page 80: Gift of Hanna Fund. Page 83: Gift of Eugene and Agnes E. Meyer. Page 84: Gift of Richard Pain in Memory of his
father. Page 92: Joachim Blauel/Artothek. Page 93: The Henry Mc Ilhenny Coll. Page 94 ht: Mr Mrs Potter Palmer Coll.
Droits réservés par l'ADAGP et la SPADEM pour les œuvres de leurs membres.

© 1994 Société Française de Promotion Artistique, 25 rue de Ponthieu, 75008 Paris. Tél. 43 59 62 00. R.C. Paris 75 B 4306
Seine. Direction de la publication: C. Lecocq. Commission paritaire: 55084 - ISSN 1242-9198. Dépôt légal: 2ème trimestre 1994.
Imprimé par ISTRA-BL Strasbourg. Photogravure: Clin d'œil, Vanves et Cliché-Union, Montrouge.

92